Time to WRITE

More Than 100 Professional Writers Reveal
How to Fit Writing into Your Busy Life

Kelly L. Stone

adamsmedia
Avon, Massachusetts

Published by
Adams Media, an F+W Publications Company
57 Littlefield Street, Avon, MA 02322 U.S.A.
www.adamsmedia.com

ISBN 10: 1-58969-438-3
ISBN 13: 978-1-59869-438-3

Printed in Canada.

J I H G F E D C B A

Library of Congress Cataloging-in-Publication Data
is available from the publisher.

This publication is designed to provide accurate and authoritative information with regard to the subject matter covered. It is sold with the understanding that the publisher is not engaged in rendering legal, accounting, or other professional advice. If legal advice or other expert assistance
is required, the services of a competent professional person should be
sought.
—From a *Declaration of Principles* jointly adopted by a Committee of the
American Bar Association and a Committee of Publishers and Associations

Many of the designations used by manufacturers and sellers to distinguish
their product are claimed as trademarks. Where those designations appear
in this book and Adams Media was aware of a trademark claim, the designations have been printed with initial capital letters.

This book is available at quantity discounts for bulk purchases.
For information, please call 1-800-289-0963.

For Sasha and Bonaparte

Contents

Acknowledgments

I wish to thank the following people: All of the writers quoted in this book, for so generously giving of your time, ideas, and hard-earned wisdom. I thank each of you from the bottom of my heart. My agent, Jennifer DeChiara, and my editor, Jennifer Kushnier. My mother, who sacrificed many of her own dreams in life to ensure that I'd have the opportunity to pursue mine. My late father, who taught me to cherish books and reading. My brother, for always believing in me. I miss you. My sister, for being there. The many friends who have spoken words of encouragement over the years: Melanie Walrath, Susan Walrath, Melissa Knight, Dan Bellor, Susan Sullivan, Jane Ferguson, Pat Wells, Franklin Abbott, Emily Simerly, Barbara Locascio, Craig Storlie, Jill Knueppel, Ladonna Benedict, Rhonda Berry, Diana Gordick, Sallie Boyles, and Shannon Wilder. Last but not least, Robert, for many years of unfaltering support. I couldn't have done it without you.

Foreword

by Kelly James-Enger

Writing seems like the easiest thing in the world. Chances are you already have an idea you want to explore. Maybe it's the outline for a mystery you carry around in your head, or an essay about growing up you've wanted to get down for years. Or maybe you want to write for magazines or pen a children's book.

You've thought about it. You've dreamed about it. You've fantasized about seeing your work in print. So…why aren't you writing?

You're too busy. You're too tired. You're brain-dead at the end of the day. You're afraid you have nothing to say. Your kids need you. Your partner needs you. Your spider plants need you. You're afraid you'll fail. You're afraid you'll succeed. You're afraid your work won't be good enough. You don't think you'll ever get published. So it's easier to put it off and instead fantasize about the day you'll find the time and finally pursue your writing dreams.

If this sounds like you, you need this book. Kelly L. Stone interviewed dozens of successful writers—many of them best-selling authors—and discovered that they had a number of attributes in common. They also had one critical element that set them apart from the would-be writers. The successful writers didn't just talk about writing, or think about writing, or dream about writing. They actually (gasp!) wrote.

And you can too. One of the first hurdles to get over is the idea that you need huge, uninterrupted chunks of time (think months-long sabbatical) to finally tackle that novel or book of essays or to launch your freelance writing career. Be real. That's not going to happen, so ditch it as an excuse.

That's the bad news—that those long, luxurious stretches of time with nothing to do but write are a fantasy. The good news is that there is time for you to write. You just have to figure out how to make the most of it.

I learned this firsthand. When I got serious about getting published, I was working more than full time as a lawyer. But I had this urge, this itch, what Kelly calls the "Burning Desire to Write." So I got up early in the morning and I wrote. During my lunch hour, at my desk, I wrote. Sitting in court, waiting for a motion call, I wrote. Lazy Sunday afternoons, instead of watching football, I wrote. And all that writing added up. I got published. You can do the same.

In addition to finding writing time, you'll also learn why it's so important to set goals. Like Kelly, I encourage writers to set two kinds of goals—outcome goals ("I want to write a novel") and production goals ("I'll write a page a day, five days a week, until I finish my draft"). She also provides writing inspiration, tips on staying focused, and ways to deal with distractions from seasoned, professional writers who were once in your shoes. They made the commitment to their Burning Desires to Write, and you'll benefit from reading what worked—and what didn't—for them.

I found myself nodding my head in agreement many times as I read this book. Why? Because I believe and agree with what Kelly shares here. I launched a full-time freelance career more than a decade ago with two published clips. I had no connections in the publishing world, no experience, no journalism background, and no clue. But I made the commitment. I set goals. I made the most of my time, seeking ways to work more efficiently, get my work published, and make a living as a full-time freelancer. Along the way, I published two novels, hit the six-figure mark as a freelancer, and have been fortunate to teach hundreds of other writers. And much of that advice can be found in the pages that follow.

I believe succeeding as a writer has less to do with innate talent and more to do with commitment, dedication, and willingness to put the time in. But you don't have to launch your writing career alone. You've got the advice of dozens of writers just waiting for you in the pages that follow. They too had family and work obligations. They too were rejected. They too were waylaid by distractions, were afraid that their work wasn't good enough, and that they might fail. They too struggled to stay motivated and committed to their writing.

But they kept plugging—and they succeeded. Follow their advice, honor your own Burning Desire to Write, and you can too.

Kelly James-Enger is the author of six books, including *Six-Figure Freelancing: The Writer's Guide to Making More Money* and the novels, *Did You Get the Vibe?* and *White Bikini Panties*; contact her at *www.becomebodywise.com*

chapter one

No Matter How Busy You Are, You Can Find Time to Write

he secret to becoming a successful writer is this: there is no secret. You don't need an inside connection to the publishing business. You don't need a mountain cabin that allows you to hide yourself from the world in order to write your novel. You don't need extraordinary talent. Most important, you don't need huge amounts of time to get your writing done. Even if you hold down a job, have a family, care for elderly parents, or simply manage the dozens of life obligations that are required of most adults in our society, there are ways to make your writing dreams come true no matter how busy you are or what your writing goals are. This book will show you how.

I wrote this book because I dreamed of becoming a writer all my life, but I never pursued it because I didn't think I had time. I had a job, a home, a family. Yet whenever I went to the bookstore, I'd pick up a novel by a new author, read the short biography on the dust jacket, and wonder how the writer had managed to pull it off. I began to ponder how someone with a job, family, and other obligations could find time to write and do it consistently enough to become successful.

To answer that question, I went straight to the source—I interviewed 104 bestselling novelists, nonfiction book authors, magazine writers, and freelance journalists. The professional writers I interviewed *know* how to make time to write: more than thirty of the fiction authors, like Sandra Brown, Cherry Adair, and Jodi Picoult, authored *New York Times* bestsellers. More than a dozen, like Ann Major and Tara Taylor Quinn, are *USA Today* bestselling authors. Others, such as Susan Grant, Barbara Samuel, and Robyn Carr, are literary award winners. Some, like Rebecca York (pen name of Ruth Glick), are all three.

The majority of the nonfiction freelance writers quoted in this book, such as Cecil Murphey and Victor D. Chase, make a full-time living by writing, but they didn't start out that way. They had to make time to write, in spite of their busy lives. I'm going to show you how they did it so that you can do it too.

Drawing on my twenty years of experience as a professional counselor, I queried these writers about their work habits, how they found time to write while also holding down a job, what writing schedules they used, how they set and accomplished writing goals, and how they dealt with distractions. Essentially, I asked a series of questions designed to find out the ways they had become successful writers.

Not only were they all exceedingly generous with their time and information, which made interviewing them a sheer pleasure, but what they revealed was very encouraging. Not a single writer I interviewed got a lucky break. Not one of them was discovered. None of them knew someone who owned a publishing business; none of them had inside connections to the industry.

Most important, none of them had an independent source of income that freed up all their time so that they could write.

What they did have were very practical strategies for making time to write within the context of a typical, busy life. These strategies are practical and so easy to use that you can implement them immediately. I share these writers' advice and how-I-did-it stories with you to help you discover how you can make time to write and become a successful writer too.

> **"I wrote at every single given opportunity."**
>
> Sandra Brown,
> *New York Times* bestselling author

This book will help anyone who wants to find time to write. It will help you if your goal is to get published and eventually earn your main income through writing. It will also help those who want to write a novel in their leisure time or essays, poetry, or articles after work or on weekends. The strategies presented for finding time to write will help any aspiring author, whether you choose to eventually share your writing with others or not.

A Quick Overview

As you are reading, you'll find time and motivational strategies that are easy to use and effective. They are based on the advice of the professional writers I interviewed, and the sound psychological principles I've developed and applied to my own writing career.

We'll first take a look at what motivates a person to start writing. You'll hear from bestselling authors such as Christine Feehan and Steve Berry on this topic. I'll bet there will be many comments from these successful authors that you can relate to in your own life.

You'll discover that some writers started writing because the creative process brings emotional comfort to them. Bestselling author Kathryn Harrison and others will share thoughts about this aspect of becoming a writer.

We'll also take a brief look at professional writers' backgrounds. You'll find there is every type of life environment represented. There are stay-at-home moms, lawyers, doctors, airline pilots, teachers, martial arts instructors; the list goes on and on. Successful writers are people just like you and me. The basic characteristics of a successful writer are an overriding desire to write and the ability to stick with it. I'm willing to bet that the only significant difference between you and them is that they consistently find time to write. Whether it is Jennifer Blake, Pamela Morsi, or Catherine Coulter, all of these writers have to *make* time to write, and I'll show you how they do it.

You'll discover that time management is the key. No matter how hectic your life, with an effective time-management strategy, you *will* have time to write.

I'll show you the importance of creating a writing schedule and then present a variety of professional writing routines that work for such bestselling authors as Sabrina Jeffries, Rick Mofina, and many others. With the diversity of schedules I present, you'll find one or more that will work for you.

You'll learn about writing goals and why those are critical to your success. I'll teach you an easy way to set goals that are guaranteed to work. I'll present information from bestselling authors Carly Phillips, Tess Gerritsen, and others on how they set and reach their own writing goals. Based on all that good advice, I'll show you an easy way to create a writing action plan that is designed to get you to your desk and writing consistently.

I'll also present fresh ideas from writers such as Carla Neggers and Debbie Macomber for rejuvenating your inspiration to write (because when you feel inspired, you naturally want to make the time to write). We'll look at ways that the professionals have coped with issues that impact a person's motivation for making time to write, such as rejection, feeling discouraged, and writer's block.

We'll tackle the issue of dealing with interruptions and distractions that intrude on your precious writing time. Bestselling authors like Wendy Corsi Staub will provide concrete examples of how they manage to make time to write while also caring for children. L.A. Banks, Rhonda Pollero, and other bestselling authors will discuss ways to effectively set boundaries with family, friends, and neighbors who don't understand that when you are writing, you're working.

Other issues you'll hear the professionals discuss are strategies to balance family and leisure time with writing, how to tap into a virtually bottomless well of story ideas, and how they use rewards for managing the sacrifices that are inherent in becoming a successful writer.

By the time you finish this book, you will have the tools and techniques of more than one hundred successful authors to show you that there is always *time to write*.

chapter two

The Burning Desire to Write

Writers are steeped in mystery. Who are those people who write the books and articles that the rest of us read, whose names fill our bookshelves, whose characters come alive and whisk us away to other worlds, or whose nonfiction books inform, educate, and inspire us to new heights? What are the motivations, backgrounds, and experiences of the people behind the names on the spines and the smiling pictures on the dust jackets?

In this chapter, you'll hear from bestselling authors such as Sandra Brown and Julia London. You'll see that successful writers come from all walks of life. They have a wide range of experiences. In many cases, people who become successful writers have no special training or preparation for writing; they simply have a dream and pursue it. They consistently make time to write. What motivates and inspires them to make this time is a *Burning Desire to Write.*

Motivational speaker and author Napoleon Hill devoted his life to learning about and teaching others the foundations and principles required for success in any endeavor. The first element required, he discovered, is what he termed a "Burning Desire." This desire—a persistent vision that inspires action to reach an end goal—becomes the driving force that motivates a person to do the necessary tasks to achieve success in any area.

Writers Have to Write

Among the authors I interviewed, the key characteristic that they share is the need to write. Writing is something that they simply *have* to do, and because of this relentless burn to put their stories on paper, they are motivated to find time to write. Indeed, they are drawn to the written word, and they have the constant urge to get their own thoughts into written form. Their Burning Desire to Write causes them to yearn for writing whenever they aren't doing it, and writing is what they want to do most of the time. Their Burning Desire has helped them discover techniques and strategies for creating time to write so that they can fulfill that need. When you finish reading this book, you will have the tools necessary to fulfill your own Burning Desire to Write.

That's right, you also have that Burning Desire—it's the reason you picked up this book. This Burning Desire may show itself to you in that special feeling you get after you write, when you experience that deep satisfaction that nothing but writing can bring you. You feel settled, content. You have to write. When you don't write, you feel restless, agitated, and like things aren't quite okay. That's the Burning Desire to Write. It's the driving force that motivates successful authors to put pen to paper, and it's the flame that keeps them—and will keep you—finding and making time to write, over and over again.

The Burning Desire to Write manifests itself in writers even before dreams of publication are on the horizon. "I couldn't *not* write," says Jodi Picoult, bestselling author of *My Sister's Keeper* and *Nineteen Minutes*. "I would write whenever I could, because the stories batting around in my head needed to get out. I'd do a bit of work at my job, then close the door and pull out the manuscript I was working on instead. I always knew I'd be a writer, I just never really expected to be a published one."

> **"Writing is like breathing to me."**
>
> Vicki Lewis Thompson,
> *New York Times* bestselling author

This overwhelming urge to write is a driving force that will only be fulfilled by the act of writing. Successful writers simply feel better about themselves when they bow to their Burning Desire. "It was a childhood thing," says Rick Mofina, bestselling author of *Every Fear* and *A Perfect Grave*. "It wasn't directly a dream to be published. I mean, that was always there. I'm not going to say it wasn't. But I always felt the need to write every day. It didn't feel like a complete day unless I created a story or typed a sentence."

The Burning Desire to Write expresses itself in different ways. For Steve Berry, bestselling author of *The Amber Room*, it is a relentless inner voice. He says that he began writing, and still writes, just to silence the voice. "People ask me all the time, 'Why do you write?' The answer's simple—because I have to. The little voice tells me to do it, and when I do it, the voice shuts up. When I don't write, it nags at me."

The Need to Write Begins Early

This need to write starts in childhood, and it usually begins with a love of books and reading. It stays with a writer for the rest of his or her life. "I have loved stories and books as long as I can remember them being in the world," says award-winning author of *Lady Luck's Map of Vegas* and *Madame Mirabou's School of Love,* Barbara Samuel. "I loved fairy tales and songs before I could read, and once I figured out that there were people who did this for a living, there was no other career choice possible. I started writing novels in fifth grade language class, and have had a book in progress ever since."

Many writers feel that the act of writing completes them; it is as necessary to their lives as breathing. They believe that writing makes them whole, that it rounds out their day in a satisfactory way.

"It's one thing to say, 'I want to write,' it's another to say, 'I *have* to write,'" says Stephanie Losee, a freelance writer and co-author of *Office Mate: The Employee Handbook for Finding—and Managing—Romance on the Job.* That statement sums up the concept of the Burning Desire to Write.

Writers Love to Tell Stories

Writers-to-be love hearing and telling good stories. This naturally progresses into creating their own stories that they preserve by writing down. As the years pass, the love of spinning yarns blossoms into a Burning Desire to Write.

That's how it began for Christine Feehan, bestselling author of *Deadly Game.* "When I first started writing, I was a child. I loved books and read books every chance I got. If I wasn't reading, I would be writing," she says. "When I got home from school, I would pick up a pen and write because it was kind of a compulsion."

Feehan says that she had no intention, at first, to pursue publication. She simply loved to make up stories. "I didn't try very hard to get my work published. I didn't think about it for years," she says. "I was in another profession—I was a martial arts instructor—so I was basically writing for myself and enjoying it. It was my escape."

Sometimes a love of classic literature can set the stage for the Burning Desire to Write to appear later in life. "I think in the back of my mind I always thought, 'Gee, wouldn't it be wonderful to write a story like *Jane Eyre* and have it read one hundred fifty years later, and loved just as much as ever?'" says Sandra Brown, bestselling author of *Ricochet*, *Envy*, and other novels.

The inspiration of the classics was also the seed of the Burning Desire to Write for bestselling author Pamela Morsi, author of *The Cotton Queen* and other novels. "Books were a very big part of my life as a young person, so it was my version of *when I grow up I want to be a rock star*," she says. "I really wanted to be Louisa May Alcott, Laura Ingalls Wilder, or Katherine Anne Porter. I wanted to be one of those people, and that never really changed all the time I was in high school."

Writers Are Insatiable Readers

Writers can't get enough of books. If they aren't writing, they're reading, especially as children. Writers-to-be sometimes plunge themselves into make-believe worlds as a way of escaping into fantasy.

Books were an escape in childhood for Jenna Black, author of *Watchers in the Night.* "I grew up feeling very isolated, and books were always my refuge," she says. "I read voraciously from as early as I can remember."

A rich fantasy life is another common characteristic of writers. Sometimes, what inspires a rich fantasy life is a less-than-ideal childhood. Indeed, studies suggest that an unstable upbringing can lay the groundwork for creativity in adulthood, because it causes a person to turn to imaginative ways of expressing feelings.

> **"The burning desire to see my book in print kept me motivated."**
>
> Cherry Adair, *New York Times* bestselling author

As the respite and fulfillment created by the make-believe worlds of books grows, it fuels the need to write. Kathryn Harrison, the bestselling author of *Envy* and *The Seal Wife*, turned to books for comfort as a young girl. She grew up as an only child with maternal grandparents and spent a lot of time alone, reading. She read to ease a sense of emotional pain and dislocation. "The discovery of narratives like *A Little Princess*, by Frances Hodgson Burnett, or *David Copperfield* by Dickens, taught me the solace of following a hero, or heroine, through tribulations to the end," she says. "There was a great deal of hope as well as pleasure and company in that experience, and when I discovered I could write, it beckoned powerfully."

Harrison adds that she doesn't remember a time when she wasn't writing in her head as a way of ordering her experience, perceiving the world, and understanding herself. That is another manifestation of the Burning Desire to Write.

Just as reading brings solace, writing can then be a way for authors to lighten others' burdens. "I write and tell stories because I want to help people forget their cares," says Kathy Carmichael, the award-winning author of *Chasing Charlie* and *Kissing Kelli*. "There have been times in my life where I survived, in part, because entertaining books saved my sanity," she says. "I write for those moments for others."

Many authors' Burning Desire to Write manifests in this way—as a need to help others and to impact others' lives in a positive way. It's a powerful motivator to become a writer. "It's not about seeing your name in print or on the spine of a book as much as it is knowing you're affecting other people's lives in some way," says Kristina Grish, a freelance writer, nonfiction book author, and contributing editor at *Marie Claire* magazine. Grish says that it's rewarding to her to hear readers say she has influenced their lives.

The Only Requirement to Be a Writer: The Burning Desire

One of the myths about writers is that they have some type of extraordinary talent or secret training to become writers. While innate talent never hurts, the truth is professional writers have diverse and ordinary backgrounds that in many cases are not writing related. It's the Burning Desire to Write, coupled with the dedication that the desire naturally fosters, that creates a writer.

The Burning Desire to Write is fueled by different things for different people, but the end result is the same: it is the driving force that inspires a person to do whatever is necessary to make time to write and to follow through with his or her writing aspirations.

For example, Joan Wolf, author of *His Lordship's Desire* and other novels, started writing while she was a stay-at-home mom.

She simply picked up a pen, carved out a set time every day, and started writing. "When my children were not yet in school, I got a babysitter from three o'clock to five o'clock and went to the Milford public library to write five days a week. I wrote my first twelve books in longhand at the library," she says. Writing twelve books in longhand is a good example of the level of dedication that the Burning Desire to Write can inspire in a person.

If you struggle with the issue of how to make time to write because a full-time job is bogging you down, take heart. Many writers achieve success while working in traditional careers, myself included. That's because no matter what you do during the day or for a job, the Burning Desire to Write never goes away. As an aspiring author, you may already know this to be true. Ask yourself this question: do you like yourself better on the days that you do write versus the days that you don't? That's your Burning Desire to Write.

A good example of this is Kimberla Lawson Roby, the best-selling author of *Changing Faces* and *Love & Lies*. She set her sights on becoming a writer while working as a financial analyst for city government. Notice how her Burning Desire to Write manifested itself in the longing to work at something that she loved, even if she wasn't earning money. "I was inspired to become a writer about a year or so before starting this particular position, and it had a lot to do with the fact that I wanted to do something I loved, but on my own," she says. "I started thinking, 'What would I enjoy doing every single day, even if I wasn't being paid to do it?'"

Some writers have juggled multiple roles while establishing their writing careers. Their need to nurture their creative side fuels this. Bestselling author of *My Favorite Earthling*, Susan Grant, worked as an airline pilot and was also the mother of two before she became a writer. Even after publishing nine books, Grant still works as a pilot, but she has also become a successful writer. "The flying was exciting, but it didn't stimulate my creative side," she says. "I felt like I needed something. I was looking for something. I said, 'Let me start writing and see what happens.'"

Another way the Burning Desire can manifest is by creating a certain amount of discomfort at having to maintain traditional employment because the writer inside wants to be writing. The good news is that the Burning Desire to Write motivates a person to make time to do so. It inspires those who hold down jobs to find time to write.

"The fear of being stuck in a dead-end job for the rest of my life motivated the hell out of me," says Julia London, bestselling author of *The Hazards of Hunting a Duke*. London says that in order to reinvent herself and live the rest of her life doing something she loved, she wrote at night and on weekends and chased her dream of becoming a writer. What created this dedication was her Burning Desire to Write.

Seeking an outlet for his Burning Desire to Write was how freelancer Randy Southerland began his career. He started doing freelance writing while he still had a full-time job in public relations. He says that writing was a way of finding self-expression. "I was really bored doing the same thing over and over," he says. "I worked for an academic institution, and I liked the diversity that was offered by freelance writing—writing about different people and subjects."

No matter what your daily environment, if you yearn to find time to write, please be encouraged, because many people have done it while holding down jobs and juggling multiple responsibilities. Because of your Burning Desire, you are motivated to make time to write. And that time can be made by following the strategies and techniques in this book.

Writers are Creative High Achievers

The Burning Desire to Write also manifests by making most writers what motivation theorists call creative high achievers. There are some common characteristics of creative high achievers that you will probably recognize in yourself. Creative high achievers:

- **Seek out solitude on a regular basis.** They enjoy time alone to develop their talents.
- **Have vivid imaginations.** A no-brainer when it comes to writers! Many creative people were avid readers as children and used fantasy to cope with problems or trauma in their lives.
- **Are real go-getters.** They shake things up; they take calculated risks. As creative people succeed in their endeavors, they seek out even more challenging goals and push themselves in new directions.
- **Don't follow the crowd.** They seek their own way in life and are more open to exploring unknown territory.
- **Shoot for the moon.** They set challenging but achievable goals. If the goal is too low, high achievers don't feel challenged. If the goal is too high and they reach it, high achievers feel that chance played a part in their victory. Challenging themselves adequately makes high achievers believe that their efforts alone created their success.

Successful Writers Write No Matter What

Another key characteristic I discovered in my interviews with these successful authors is that many of them, in addition to carving out time to write on a regular basis, also learned to adapt to less-than-ideal writing situations when they needed to out of necessity. They embraced the mindset that successful writers write *no matter what.*

"I often say that I can write anytime, and anywhere," says Carla Neggers, the bestselling author of *The Widow.* "I think it's easy to think that everything has to be perfect—you have to have the house to yourself, you have to have the right equipment, that everything has to be perfect in order to sit down and write. I see that delaying people sometimes."

Do you see yourself in that statement? Do you believe that everything has to be perfect before you can write? If so, use the sentence, *Successful writers write no matter what,* as a mantra, and repeat it often to yourself as you read this book. With obvious exceptions for illness and genuine emergencies, adopting this mindset will help you focus on what you need to do to get to your desk and write, rather than focusing on all the obstacles to writing.

This doesn't mean that if you need certain conditions in which to write creatively that you abandon that need. There will be strategies in this book for helping you maximize the time when your creativity is at its peak. What it does mean, though, is that incorporating writing time into day-to-day life is a hallmark of any successful writer, whether that means getting in an hour of writing before heading to work, on your lunch break while at work, while the baby is napping, or simply writing around, in between, and despite of all of your daily tasks. This book will show you how to do all of those things.

Psychology 101: Successful Writers Believe They Can Write

If you believe that finding success as a writer is beyond the scope of your abilities, you're not alone. Even accomplished authors struggle with the idea that they couldn't make it as a writer—at first.

Thinking that ordinary folks couldn't become writers almost prevented Roxanne St. Claire, author of *Thrill Me to Death* and other bestselling novels, from becoming the successful writer she is today. "I had to let go of the debilitating belief that mere mortals cannot write a book," she says. "Once I realized that, nothing could stop me, because I believe in my deepest heart that I was put on this earth to tell my stories and entertain readers."

Acknowledging that you have that belief, that writing is something you simply *must* do, is how you overcome thinking that you can't succeed or that there's no time to write. You have to accept the fact that if you want to become a writer, and you are willing to devote the energy necessary to make that happen, then you can do it. All of the writers quoted in this book started out where you may be today: unpublished and with only a dream in the heart. But they did it, and you can too.

Successful writers have also struggled with the issue of feeling that what they had to say wasn't important enough to warrant writing. JoAnn Ross, bestselling author of *No Safe Place*, had to overcome this. "One of my many college majors was literature, and for several years I doubted I could write a novel because I'd never be Tolstoy. It finally dawned on me that the world already had a Tolstoy, and it didn't need another one. Which is when I decided to tell my stories my way," she says.

Successful authors in many cases begin writing by simply honoring their Burning Desire to Write, even in the face of self-doubt. "If I had thought of it as, 'Was I qualified?' instead of honoring the thing that came alive inside me, I would have never done this," says Charlene Ann Baumbich, author of the *Dearest Dorothy* series.

This is why making time to write is so important; it's too easy to talk yourself out of it. You must simply decide that you will be a writer and begin. "When I decided to try my hand at writing, I had no idea how to do it or how long it took," says novelist Pamela Morsi. "So I gave myself ten years to turn out a book. That sounds silly to me now, but I didn't know. It took me about a year and a half. I just kept writing and writing and writing."

Writers write because it's in their blood; it's a part of who they are. Without writing, they would feel lost. "I love [being a writer]," says Beverly Barton, bestselling author of *The Dying Game*. "I cannot imagine doing anything else. Writing is what I do. It's my job. But it is also who I am."

You probably see yourself within these pages and the writers' stories. That means that somewhere inside you there's a successful writer who's ready to come out.

chapter three

The Secret to Finding Time to Write

*M**any aspiring writers believe* writing is an activity that has to be done away from the family, the job, and daily life. They think that if they can't flee to a secluded mountain cabin and hide from their responsibilities, then writing can't be done. Yet my interviews revealed that successful writers, like bestselling author Tara Taylor Quinn, take the opposite approach—they adapt writing *into* their lives. For these writers, writing isn't simply a task or a job, it's a lifestyle. Writing as a lifestyle means that you weave writing into the fabric of your existing routine; you make room for it in your day. Overwhelmingly, professional writers do this by using schedules.

In this chapter, we'll look at the writing schedule. We'll examine why it's important to the creative process and how it supports writing as a habit. When writing becomes your habit, it becomes part of your lifestyle. It also helps you hold yourself accountable to your writing time. The first step in learning how to schedule writing into your day is understanding and prioritizing your daily needs.

Psychology 101: A New Way of Looking at Time Management

Abraham Maslow was a humanistic psychologist in the 1940s who developed a theory of human achievement based on five levels of needs. He arranged these needs into a hierarchy to demonstrate that each level's needs must be met before a person can move to the one above it. Ideally, the individual meets all of their lower- and middle-tier needs and reaches the top of the hierarchy, which is self-actualization or self-fulfillment.

Imagine a triangle divided into five tiers. At the first tier, or the very bottom of the triangle, are your physiological needs, such as hunger and thirst. These needs must be met first before the needs above them can be addressed. An example of this is when you are sitting in a meeting at work thirty minutes before lunch. Rather than focusing on the task at hand, you're trying to decide where you're going to eat. The physiological needs comprise the widest and largest section of the triangle because most people spend the majority of their time fulfilling them. In other words, you spend most of your time in activities that allow you to buy groceries, keep a roof over your head, and put shoes on your kids' feet.

Safety needs, such as security, stability, and order, comprise the second level. This means that after the physiological needs are met, people then need to feel safe and make sense of the world and their own personal experience within the world. It's hard to become self-actualized if you feel that your safety is threatened in any way.

The third level is the need for belonging and love, and the fourth level reflects esteem needs, which are the desire for success and self-respect. Everyone wants to feel appreciated for their efforts. The fifth and top level indicates a person's need for self-actualization or self-fulfillment, where the individual strives to meet his or her full potential. Self-actualization, or self-fulfillment, manifests in different ways for different people, but for writers, it usually means fulfilling their burning desire to write.

Maslow's hierarchy of needs can be viewed as a task prioritization table. It shows that if you create a plan for meeting your first four levels of needs, then fulfilling your Burning Desire to Write is assured. Using a schedule,

> **"First of all, you have to set a schedule. Whatever that is, you have to set it and stick to it."**
>
> Karen Asp, freelance writer

with its inherent time-management strengths, will help you do this. You will be able to meet the necessities of life *and* find time to write.

Why You Need a Writing Schedule

Marking time to write on your existing schedule automatically makes space for it in your day while you also conduct your basic need activities. Using a writing schedule lets you, your family, and the world know that writing is important. All of these elements lead to consistent writing, which in turn creates opportunities for success.

The successful authors interviewed for this book found that writing schedules are an important first step to making time to write. Tara Taylor Quinn, the bestselling author of *In Plain Sight* and *Behind Closed Doors*, says that before she got established as a professional writer she set aside time to write every day around her other daily activities. "I was more flexible then as I had other responsibilities that sometimes had to take momentary priority, but I always looked at my week, and at each individual day, and before the week began I knew what time slots during the week I would be writing," she says.

Quinn stresses that she never wavered from those time slots unless there was a major emergency. "This set a habit not only for my own psyche, but for the minds of those around me too," she says. "I was reasonable about the time I set aside, I made sure I was tending to my other roles and duties—but my writing time was sacred. I couldn't be talked out of it."

Planning ahead like Quinn did is essential to making time to write. Waiting for the right time to simply appear in your busy day is a guaranteed way to ensure that you won't write because something else will come up. Someone will call, or you'll get engrossed in a television program, or any number of other daily distractions that vie for your attention will crop up. Suddenly, it'll be time for bed and you discover that another day has passed and you haven't written.

That's why you need a predetermined writing schedule, because you want to make writing part of your existing routine. A schedule gives it the same importance as your other must-do activities. Just like grocery shopping, picking up the kids from daycare, and putting in the hours at your job, writing will become part of the natural flow of your day when you schedule it.

A Schedule Makes Writing a Habit

Your focus as an aspiring writer trying to find time to write should be on creating the writing habit, and using a schedule is the magic key. A habit is an action that we take on a frequent basis, without conscious thought; it is ingrained in our behavior patterns so deeply that it requires no deliberate intent to perform. Most people tend to think of habits as bad because those are the only ones you talk about: you want to stop smoking, you want your husband to stop leaving wet towels on the bathroom floor. However, habits cover all sorts of activities, not all of them bad—automatically stopping your car at red lights is a good habit, for example. Habits form because it's a way the mind frees up your attention to focus on things that are more pressing at any given moment.

When writing becomes a habit, it becomes an automatic space holder in your day. You want to form the habit that at such-and-such a time on Monday, Wednesday, and Saturday (or whatever schedule you end up choosing in the next chapter), you can't go shopping, you can't take lunch with friends, and you can't chat on the phone for an hour with your Aunt Bessie because *that's your writing time.*

Once writing is a habit, the misperception that you don't have time to write disappears. You *do* have time: it's right there on your schedule.

Many writers write every day. Even if it's not for a long time, if you can spend some time at your desk every day, that goes a long way toward making writing a habit. Bestselling novelist Julia London says that this is the reason that she tries to touch some part of her writing daily. "It may be nothing more than editing a sentence or two, or it may be writing pages and pages that I will toss out later," she says. "If I write every day, then writing becomes a habit, and the time becomes natural."

Writing every day is the ideal, but not everyone can do that because of various obligations. Fortunately, daily writing isn't necessary to form the habit. However, consistent writing *is* necessary to form the habit. Habits form by repetition. The more you repeat the action, the more it moves to the realm of unconscious habit. The essential element here is that you create a writing schedule and you stick to it. If you only write two days a week, for example, you'll still form the writing habit, it'll just take a little longer.

Because Gemma Halliday, author of the *High Heel Mysteries*, started writing while she had another occupation, she was unable to write every day. Her strategy was to schedule in writing a couple of hours per week and then follow through. "Before I began writing full time, it was harder to fit in writing and life, but I always tried to keep some kind of consistent schedule up, even if it was just a couple of hours a week," she says. "At least then I knew that I had those two hours and could be plotting in my head until I had a chance to actually put the scene to paper."

While daily writing is the ideal, simply showing up to write at your scheduled time, however often that is, honors your Burning Desire and develops discipline. Discipline and making yourself show up at the desk consistently makes writing a habit; it makes it part of your lifestyle. Those are both critical strategies for success.

The more often you can make *time to write* a space holder in your day, the more writing will become a habit. You'll get to your desk at the appointed time because that's just what you do. Just like you automatically get up at a certain time every day and start doing the tasks necessary to begin your day, time to write will become an automatic activity that is blended into your routine naturally.

The concept of writing as a habit is clearly demonstrated by bestselling novelist Carly Phillips, author of *Simply Sexy* and *Brazen*, when she says, "I believe you have to carve out writing time and treat it as precious except for emergencies. I also believe you have to apply yourself. It's too easy to find other things to do!"

In other words, the habit will manifest itself if you keep at it. You identify your time to write, and then the habit of writing will form the more you follow through. You reinforce this habit by keeping your scheduled writing appointment, and when you sit at your desk (or in front of your notebook or laptop at the library or park) at the designated time, you *write*. You don't compose e-mail, you don't watch television, and you don't blow it off for a nap. When you reinforce writing as a habit, success will follow.

Lori Handeland, the bestselling author of *Rising Moon*, formed the habit by diligently sticking to her schedule. "I do not go to lunch. I do not volunteer for anything, unless it's outside those hours," she says. "If I were a lawyer or doctor or a cosmetics salesperson, I couldn't run a bake sale during work hours, and I'm not doing it now."

Benefits of a Writing Schedule

Schedules create the writing habit very easily. Some writers I interviewed were so busy when they first began their writing careers that they scheduled every activity in their lives. In situations like this, where you are extremely pressed for time, a schedule is even more critical to success.

Maxine Rock, a freelance writer, worked as a teacher, raised a family, and started her writing career all at the same time. She did it by budgeting time for every single task she had to juggle, including writing. "Everything was a deadline," she says, "everything from picking up the children at daycare to getting food on the table at the right time to getting the manuscript in to correcting my students' papers. Every moment was budgeted and accounted for."

Schedules Help You Write No Matter What

In the last chapter I told you that one of the characteristics of the successful authors I interviewed is that they write no matter what. Using a schedule is how they do that. To them, they've written on a schedule for so long and so consistently that it has become a habit. It's routine. It's a natural part of what they do. Getting to the desk to write is *automatic*.

That's what you're striving to accomplish as well. Writing needs to become a habit. Habits are formed and strengthened only by repetition. When you have a concrete schedule in front of you, you are driven to fulfill the schedule, and each time you follow through on it, your writing habit gets stronger.

Of course, you need to be flexible enough to alter your schedule in order to deal with true emergencies, but thankfully those are rare. It's the *daily* distractions that are the bane of the developing writer: the e-mails, the chatty neighbors, the bills that need paying, the grass that needs cutting, the kitchen floor that needs mopping. Schedules give you a genuine reason to say you've got something else to do right now because it's your writing time. *Writing* as a permanent space holder in your day will give you the mental motivation to get to your desk. Schedules help you say no to those daily distractions. The flexibility of schedules can also help you write no matter what. When people think of schedules, they tend to think of rigid structures like TV listings, doctor's appointments, or meetings at work. However, in reality, all schedules are flexible. How many times has your favorite program been pre-empted for a special sports event, or the doctor was running late due to another emergency, or a meeting at work was pushed back by an hour because someone was handling another problem that came up at the last minute? Not often, but it does happen.

There will be rare times when you have to be flexible with your writing schedule—perhaps you'd planned on writing for an hour but you get called in to work, or your hot water heater breaks, or your child becomes ill. In situations like that, what the professional writers I interviewed try to do is keep some semblance of their writing schedule, even if they get in less time than they had originally planned. Maybe they scheduled sixty minutes of writing but only got in thirty. At least they got that thirty minutes done. "We wrote every day, no matter what, even if the amount wasn't always what we wanted to do and real life crept in," says Joyce and Jim Lavene, authors of the Sharyn Howard mystery series.

The beauty of a schedule is that it gives you the willpower to write no matter what. I recently demonstrated this power in my own career. I had scheduled time to edit this chapter and had arranged to have a quiet house to work in (which is my preference). Instead, just as I was sitting down to the only two hours I had that day to work on the book, roofers showed up unexpectedly at my home to repair a problem.

At first, I thought, "Well, that's it. I can't get my work done." But I was under a deadline. I reminded myself that successful writers write no matter what. I had *scheduled* a block of time as writing time. So I edited this chapter with banging, drilling, and shouting going on over my head. Having writing time marked out on my daily calendar helped me focus on the work rather than the obstacle to the work (which for me was the noise).

A schedule also helps you accommodate other must-do activities along with your writing, like caring for your children when necessary. "I actually learned to write with noise around me," says novelist Christine Feehan. "I would sit there while my children were watching television and write my stories with them in the room. So I could basically write anywhere, anytime."

A Schedule Stimulates the Creative Process

There is another key benefit to using a schedule that makes it a very powerful tool: it enhances productivity. The writers I interviewed capitalize on this benefit by using writing schedules that coincide with when their creative juices are flowing.

In other words, if they know that they are more creative in the morning, that's when they schedule themselves to write. "I know people who set their alarm for three in the morning and work from three to seven," says Rhonda Pollero, the bestselling author of the Finley Anderson Tanner mystery series. "Then they get ready to go to work and do their job. I know other people who don't kick in until three in the afternoon. So I think it's whatever your body clock tells you is your more creative time."

The nice thing about a schedule is that you can fine-tune it to match your individual creative process. Most writers can pinpoint when their creativity is flowing, and they take advantage of this time by using the power of the schedule. But because schedules are flexible, it means that not only can you adjust it when you need to tend to some other obligation, it also means that when the words are really flowing, you can add additional writing time into your routine too. "I begin work every morning between eight and ten," says Sandra Marton, a top author for *Harlequin Presents*, "although when the energy's really pumping, I often wake long before dawn and head down to my office."

A Writing Schedule Holds You Accountable

The invisible power of a writing schedule is that it gives you a way to hold yourself accountable. It makes writing time important. It's not the "I'll do it if I have time" chore that gets shoved to the back burner every time something else comes up. Just like going to your job or cooking dinner, there may be days when you don't feel up to it, but you do it anyway. You feel better about yourself with every schedule you successfully complete because your Burning Desire to Write is being fulfilled. That motivates you to follow through the next time, which ingrains writing as a habit. That causes your writing productivity to soar.

A writing schedule also taps the power of your subconscious mind, the true source of your muse. We'll cover this more in depth in Chapter 9, but for now, understand that by writing on a schedule you are gradually building a bridge from your conscious mind to the wellspring of your creativity. The writing habit lets your mind know, "okay, it's time to write," and when that time rolls around, it's ready to spring into action. Rather than expelling your energy by wrangling with yourself about actually sitting down to write, your schedule has made the act of getting to your desk a habit; therefore, your attention is freed up to focus on creative content instead. Then, even if you only have fifteen minutes to write, you will make maximum use of that time because your creative well will be primed.

This process strengthens over time. The more you follow through on your schedule, the more writing becomes a habit, and your creative momentum builds.

A Schedule Improves Your Skills

Writing regularly on a schedule will also improve your skills as a writer. That will increase the positive feelings that you have toward writing, which in turn fuels the motivation to write again. It's a circular, win-win process.

You will also have more writing output, which will increase your opportunities for submitting work and getting published. These are experiences that freelance writer Sandra J. Gordon says she had. "I really felt like my skills gelled," she says. "The day in and day out being around words, being at my computer having to crank stuff out. I felt that really helped my freelancing too."

Psychology 101: Your Dream + Details = Your Vision of Success

Before we move on, let's pause to discuss an important psychological concept: your *Vision of Success* and why you need one.

A critical element to success in any endeavor is to begin with the end in mind. You must know in detail what it is you're striving to accomplish. One reason that people fail to reach their aspirations in life is simply due to lack of specificity about what they want. Most people tend to focus on what they *don't* want, rather than what they *do* want.

You might say, "I want to be a writer." That's fine, but you'll need to be more specific to help birth that vision into reality. What kind of writing do you want to do? What topics or types of books or articles will you pen? Do you finish a novel or your family's memoirs? Are your poems published in a specific journal? Are you writing for national women's magazines? Is writing providing your main income, or are you doing it on the side? About how much money are you earning from your writing?

Spend a few minutes thinking of your own Vision of Success with regard to writing. You might journal about it or make some notes to refer back to later as more specifics occur to you. Get as detailed of a picture as you can of where you want writing to take you.

Many professional writers utilize mental imagery and affirmations to create the motivation and inspiration to write. When you have a picture of your own success to drive and encourage you, then you will naturally feel motivated to make the time to write. Writing will find its place as one of your must-do activities at the bottom of your task prioritization table. Working toward a Vision of Success gives you a destination to move toward. Even on days that you don't feel particularly motivated to stick to your schedule (and all writers do), that vision will spur you to action.

Charge your Vision of Success by mentally generating lots of positive feelings to associate with it. Really *feel* what it will be like when you can claim your place among the ranks of successful

> "Time to write was made by stealing it from other things, such as watching television, reading, or lunching with friends."
>
> Jennifer Blake, *New York Times* bestselling author

31

writers, whatever that means for you. Frame that vision like a virtual photograph in the forefront of your mind. Draw your attention to it frequently as you go about your day. Wallow in the good feelings that it creates for you. The mental and emotional energy created by this vision will inspire you to take action toward creating it.

Creating a vision of herself as a successful writer is a technique that novelist Tara Taylor Quinn employed both before and after she was published. Notice how Quinn generates positive emotions to associate with her vision. "It was the constant visualization," she says. "I'd picture myself published. I'd daydream about it on road trips, or while I was doing the dishes. I'd think about how it would feel, what people would say, how I'd react."

Quinn still does this activity, only now with some slightly different goals. "I've hit the *USA Today* bestseller list and now I daydream about hitting the *New York Times* list—clear down to the flowers my publisher is going to send!" she says.

The Twenty-Four-Hour Time Budget

Creating a writing schedule may feel impossible to you right now because you already feel stretched to capacity. But one easy way to pinpoint exactly where you can fit in some writing time is to take a look at how you currently spend your time. You're going to discover you have much more time than you thought you did.

Keep a daily journal for one week of how you currently spend every minute of your day—just a typical Monday through Sunday. Record every minute of your day and what you're doing. Write down the time you spend in all of your activities, including job and commute time, sleeping, leisure time, e-mail/Internet time, meal preparation and cleanup, shopping, driving kids to and fro, laundry, dog walking, and so on. This will help you determine how your day-to-day hours are being spent, and you can use this exercise in the next chapter to decide on a writing schedule.

At the end of the seven days, examine each twenty-four-hour period to determine how you used that time. This exercise will give you a picture of how on a day-to-day basis you are actually spending the hours of your day. Just like recording every penny you spend will make you conscious of how many dollars you're really shelling out at the fast-food drive-through, it's likely that you will discover that you are disposing of more time than you care to in activities that you could either eliminate, compress, delegate, or double up with something else so that you can write instead.

For example, I did this exercise for a typical work day and discovered that I spent ten hours for job and commute time, eight for sleep, two hours for meal preparation and cleanup, three hours for checking e-mail, reading, and leisure time in the evening, and one hour to finish nightly chores and get ready to go to bed. I decided that three hours every night for e-mail and television was a waste, and it was also delaying my bedtime. Because I choose to write early in the morning, the only way for me to get up earlier was to get in bed sooner, so I had to compress those nightly activities into a shorter time frame. When looking at how you spend the hours of your day, you can make adjustments like I did in order to come up with a writing schedule, because this is how you find time to write.

Another way to use this exercise is to identify a period of time during your typical week when you aren't already in demand

and then claim that as your writing time. You may discover that you can rearrange tasks or delegate some duties so that you can write while others are sleeping, during breaks at work, or before your spouse arrives home in the evening. Locate some time that is already free, when you are engaging in a discretionary activity, and capitalize on it by writing. Use the most logical, available time to your advantage, advises Robyn Carr, the award-winning author of *Virgin River*. In other words, find a period of time when you wouldn't typically be in demand, and then claim that as your writing time. Since the goal is to make writing part of your lifestyle, it's okay to start small. If all you can squeeze in is thirty minutes before work, then that's when you'll be writing.

Another way to look at this time budget is to scrutinize time spent between activities. How much time do you spend in the morning between getting up and leaving for work? Do you really need one hour to get dressed, or can you iron clothes and pack lunches the night before and shorten your preparation routine so that a half hour can be used for writing instead? What about when you get home at night? Is there a half hour here and there between evening obligations that is unaccounted for? Is there some time after you've done your nightly chores and before you go to bed that you could devote to writing? Look for these kinds of patterns in your existing schedule and highlight those, because that's where your writing time is.

chapter four

Writing Schedules That Work

In the last chapter, we explored the value of schedules and how they allow you to integrate writing into your routine. Schedules make writing a habit, which in turn makes it part of your lifestyle.

In this chapter, I'll present the various innovative schedules that bestselling authors such as Rick Mofina and Eloisa James use. Just as there is a diversity of authors, there is also diversity of schedules; but all these schedules work. They will help you find time to write.

Schedule #1: The Early-Morning Writer

Those whose days are committed to family or work obligations must find time to write in hours that are not already devoted to some other activity. For many people, especially those who keep more traditional hours, the most logical, available time that they can find time to write is in the morning while others are still sleeping. Getting up early, between three and five A.M., is a common way that many people have managed to make time to write while juggling full-time responsibilities.

For instance, novelist Rick Mofina started his writing career while working as a crime reporter. Writing early in the morning before he left for work was a key to his success. Notice that he chose the Early-Morning schedule because that was when his creativity was at top form. "I forced myself to get up earlier and just carved a little time out of the day in the early hours," he says. "I was a morning writer in terms of being fresher, and the first hours were mine. I couldn't fathom how I could come home after a grueling day as a news reporter and then try to write creatively."

The Early-Morning schedule is a common and widely used strategy among successful writers. Author Kathryn Harrison says that she wrote her first novel between the hours of five and seven in the morning before she left for work.

Many writers find that the morning is when they are at peak form in terms of production, and so they set their schedule accordingly. Tim O'Shei, a freelance writer and editor, rose in the predawn hours while he was holding down a full-time job as a teacher. Again, because early morning hours were his optimal time for creativity, O'Shei diligently guarded this time against intrusions. "I set a schedule where I woke up early, between four and five A.M.," he says. "I had two or three hours of solid writing time, and I was very protective of it. I found that was my best writing time."

Benefits of the Early-Morning Schedule

For writers with young children, rising before the kids do is an effective way to balance the numerous duties of raising a family with finding time to write. The children are still asleep and do not need your attention during that time. You can focus on writing with the assurance that they are safe and sound in bed, and that immediately knocks one common distraction aside.

Nancy Christie, a freelance writer and author of *The Gifts of Change*, used this schedule when she was beginning her career and when her children were small. She would get up at four and write copy before she got her kids up.

Early-morning writing is the schedule of choice for many bestselling authors with young kids. "I had to write very early in the morning because my daughter was three and still home full time," says novelist Roxanne St. Claire, who wrote her first published book between the hours of four forty-five and seven A.M. "I simply cannot produce fresh pages when there's a child awake in the house."

The Early-Morning schedule is also beneficial if you need a quiet house in which to write, like I do. Everyone else is still in bed, the traffic outside hasn't gotten geared up yet, the world is generally calmer, and the atmosphere seems more conducive to writing.

How to Start Using the Early-Morning Schedule

If the early morning hours are the most logical, available time that you can fit writing into your busy life, here's how to begin. Start slow. Set your alarm clock backwards in five-minute increments each morning over the course of two weeks. If you normally get up at seven, then on day one you'll get up at six fifty-five; on day two, six fifty; on day three, six forty-five; and so on. Even though you'll only have a few minutes to write for the first few days, practice getting up as soon as the alarm rings (no hitting the snooze button) and go straight to your desk and start writing. Getting up a little bit earlier each day rather than trying to do it all at once will help your body and brain adjust more easily. After moving your rising time backward by five minutes for two weeks, you'll be getting up about an hour earlier. Keep going for another ten days if you want to write for two hours in the morning, and so on.

The amount of time you write in the mornings and how many days out of the week you do this are your choice. A lot will probably depend on your other obligations. Be flexible. If you have a particularly long day ahead, it's okay to adjust your rise time accordingly. Maybe you only get up thirty minutes early that day rather than one hour early. Or maybe you can only get up early three days out of five on a consistent basis due to your other obligations. That's okay too. The point is that you are carving out time to write and doing it consistently. You're putting writing on your schedule and sticking to it. That's the trick to finding time to write despite your busy life.

Other Considerations

You might have to make other accommodations when using the Early-Morning schedule. For example, you will probably have to go to bed earlier the night before, unless you can simply do without the sleep. You may have to eat dinner earlier or get your exercise in sooner in the evening. You may not be able to stay up for the eleven o'clock news anymore. Your spouse may have to help clean the kitchen at night or help the kids with their homework so that you can get in bed. Make adjustments as necessary, and start slow to give yourself and your family time to adapt.

How Your Vision of Success Helps with the Early Morning Schedule

Remember your Vision of Success that I encouraged you to create? I hope you did spend some time on that, because part of the purpose of that vision is to motivate you to get to your desk at your scheduled writing time. Your Vision of Success is what keeps you inspired to work your writing schedule, especially if you are attempting a drastic alteration in your day-to-day routine. If you decide to use the Early-Morning schedule and start writing at four A.M., yet you aren't accustomed to rising before seven, you have quite an adjustment on your hands. It's your Vision of Success that will provide the motivation that you need to follow through.

I'll give you an example from my own life. About five years ago, after reading that getting up before dawn was a common element in many successful people's lives (not just writers), I decided I would start getting up at three thirty in the morning to write before reporting to my job as a high-school counselor. I was due at work at seven, which meant I had to start getting dressed by six and be ready to leave by six thirty. If I wanted to get in two hours of writing, I needed to get up at three thirty in order to be at my desk by four. I needed thirty minutes to get coffee, feed my pets, and let my brain wake up.

> **"This is the secret to writing: a tube of super glue. You apply the glue to the seat of your pants, and then apply your pants to the seat of the chair."**
>
> Lynne Alpern, comedy writer and author of *Oh Lord, I Sound Just Like Mama*

The transition was difficult for me because I tend to just dive into something rather than easing my way into it (which is why I recommend you do it incrementally). I shifted from waking up at my usual time of six to waking up at three thirty literally overnight. It took about six months to adjust, and, truthfully, it was a painful transition. The temptation to turn the alarm off and roll over and go back to sleep was overwhelming.

The only thing that got me out of bed every time that alarm rang at three thirty was my Vision of Success. I'd lay there in the dark and ask myself, "How bad do you want to be a successful writer?" That usually got me up because I wanted it bad. I kept up this schedule of early morning writing for two hours a day, five days a week, and in two years I wrote a novel that got published and also began a successful freelance career. Despite this success, I still work as a counselor full time, so I continue this practice of early morning writing to this day. (And trust me, it does get easier the longer you do it. Nowadays, I couldn't sleep until seven A.M. even if somebody paid me.)

The strategy of calling to mind the Vision of Success is one that novelist Jenna Black used too. She's an early morning writer who carved out this specific time to write when she realized that she was going to have do everything possible to make her own writing dreams come true. "I knew that morning was my best writing time, even though I'm not a morning person, so I forced myself to wake up before sunrise every morning to work on my current project," she explains. "It meant shifting my whole schedule so that it curtailed my evening activities. But I asked myself—would I feel like I'd given my dream my best shot if I chose to, say, watch TV at night, stay up late, and wake up just in time to get myself to work the next morning? The answer was an obvious no, so I made up my mind to change my schedule."

Schedule #2: The After-Hours Writer

The opposite of the Early-Morning schedule is the After-Hours schedule. It's useful for those who feel more creative when the sun goes down. Writing after others are in bed for the night is good for those who desire quiet. Or your biological clock may cause you to feel more alert late at night versus in the predawn hours. It may be that it's the most logical, available time for you to write.

You can adapt After-Hours writing into your routine in a number of ways. If you're the first one home in the afternoons, try writing for an hour or two before your family arrives. Or if you have obligations that require your attention into the evening, schedule in writing after those are satisfied for the night. You can also schedule yourself to write after everyone else has gone to bed.

Working after her family went to bed is how Sabrina Jeffries, bestselling author of *Only a Duke Will Do* and *Beware a Scot's Revenge*, scheduled her writing time when she returned to work after the birth of her child. In fact, Jeffries wrote her first three books that way. "I had spent a couple of summers as a technical writer, which while it was a very boring job, left me with lots of energy at the end of the day. I did have to go back to work [after the baby was born], so I decided I would get a job as a technical writer and write at night," she says. Jeffries wrote after her son and husband went to bed until eleven each night. "So everything I had to get done at home I did until eight, and when eight o'clock came, that was it. I wrote."

The After-Hours writing schedule works well for those who have full-time jobs and who also have responsibilities they must tend to in the afternoons and evenings—children, for instance. Nikoo and Jim McGoldrick, a husband-and-wife writing team who've penned *The Project* and other books under the pseudonym Jan Coffey, both had other vocations when they began writing and were parents to two young boys. They wrote at night after the kids were asleep. "Jim and I both were professionals and working for many years before we got published," says Nikoo. "Our writing was always after hours. We would get home from work, and we had the children and all their activities, and so forth. We wrote from eight to midnight during the week, and then in the morning we'd get up at five and have to go to work."

After-Hours writing doesn't mean you have to write until midnight or later if that doesn't suit your lifestyle. Bestselling novelist Carmen Green, author of *Flirt* and *What a Fool Believes*, writes at night after her job and child-care duties are fulfilled. But she can still get started early enough so she has adequate time for a good night's sleep. "I get started writing about seven thirty P.M.," she says, "and I write until ten. Then I stop, I clean my writing stuff up, and I get ready for bed."

The key to success here, as with all the schedules, is to designate your writing time in advance on a regular basis, and then exercise self-discipline by following through. Put it down on your agenda book just like a "real" appointment. That's how professionals like Michelle Hoover do it. She's a freelance writer whose short story appeared in *Best New American Voices 2004*, and she also works as a professor at Boston University. She makes afternoon writing a part of her routine. "I keep my daytime very scheduled, so my afternoons are always for writing," she says.

The good news is that it doesn't have to be a lot of time. One hour, five days a week, will get you there. That's how the bestselling author of *Pleasure for Pleasure*, Eloisa James, managed to hold down employment as a professor and write her first romance novel. "I would work until four in the afternoon, then every afternoon I would write from four to five on the book," she says. "That was my routine."

How to Start Using the After-Hours Writing Schedule

Begin using the After-Hours schedule by selecting what portion of the day you'll be writing: afternoon, evening, or late night. Then decide how many days of the week you'll write, for how long, and then pencil it in. Try for time that is naturally free of obligations, perhaps when the children are doing their homework or while everyone else is watching TV.

If you have no obligation-free time, and you do not want to stay up too late due to early morning commitments, try to compress some of your nighttime activities into a shorter time frame. To do this, set an alarm clock for one week at the time that you want to start writing, then make a list of all the activities that delay you from starting at that time.

Next, make a plan for getting all of those chores done sooner. Can you get dinner on the table earlier, or can you enlist the help of your spouse or an older child to walk the dog while you load the dishwasher? If your children have homework that you need to supervise, can they get it done by a certain time? Can you multi-task more and pay bills while you're waiting for the casserole to bake or while your children are bathing? If your favorite show is on at the only time you have free to write, record it.

Notice what's preventing the delay, and actively make a plan for getting those things done earlier. This is where the discipline comes in: If you schedule yourself to write at a certain time, it's imperative that you follow through. Building the writing habit fosters self-discipline, but it's up to you to exercise that discipline.

L.A. Banks (who also writes as Leslie Esdaile Banks), bestselling author of *The Wicked* and *Vegas Bites*, balanced her family's needs with her writing by using the After-Hours schedule. Banks worked a traditional job and also met the needs of her children in the evenings. She chose to write during the time when she was previously watching television. "Where I would normally sit down and collapse and watch TV till the nightly news went off at eleven thirty, from eight to twelve, that's a good four-hour block, and that's where I would write. That's how I did it," she says.

If After-Hours writing for you means writing after the family goes to bed, or after you normally retire at night, inch your bedtime forward by five minutes every night for two weeks, while maintaining your same wake time, until you are writing for the amount of time that you desire each night.

Schedule #3: The Office Writer (Before Work, After Work, and During Scheduled Breaks)

If Early-Morning or After-Hours writing schedules aren't an option for you because you don't want to lose the sleep, or your evening obligations are simply too time-consuming to allow it, another option is to take your laptop or writing materials to your place of employment and write for an hour or two before your coworkers arrive. This is a strategy that novelist Steve Berry, who also works as an attorney, employed for over a decade. "I'd go in about six thirty or seven o'clock and write for two, two-and-a-half hours," he says. "Then I tended to my legal business after that, because I had to make a living."

Writing in the office before others get there is an effective way to make writing part of your existing lifestyle if you have a full-time job. You're out of the house, so distractions from your family or the home environment will not be a concern. Arriving early will ensure that your coworkers won't be a distraction either.

Bestselling author Cecil Murphey, who has written or collaborated on over one hundred books, was a pastor before he became a writer. He set a schedule of showing up at his office early and writing before his secretary arrived, and that made writing a daily habit for him. "When I got to my church, the first thing I did at eight was set up my typewriter and write until my secretary got there at nine," he says. "Then I moved it back to seven so I had two hours. That was great discipline."

You can also write during lunch and on scheduled breaks. If you can leave for lunch, pack a sandwich and go to a park or the library and spend some time writing. Or simply close the door to your office, let your voice mail pick up the phone, and write. You might also be able to stay an hour or two late and write after work if your lifestyle accommodates a later arrival home in the evening. Why sit in bumper-to-bumper traffic when you can write for half an hour after quitting time and arrive home at the same time anyway? The important step is to set aside some part of your workday for writing, pencil it in, and follow through on that commitment.

This schedule works for those who work inside the home too. Take your laptop or notebook to a park or the library for an hour to two every day and write before you return home to your other duties, or write between your in-home tasks.

How to Start Using the Write-at-Work Schedule

Check first to make sure that your workplace policy allows you to come in early or stay late for your own reasons. Then plan to leave your home early enough that you can arrive with adequate time to write. This will probably mean rising earlier too. As with the previous schedules, adjust your times slowly to allow yourself an adaptation period. When you arrive at your office, close the door so that any other early birds won't disturb you. Do not turn on your work computer—you might get drawn into checking e-mail and other work-related projects and lose your valuable writing time. As soon as you arrive, open your laptop or notebook and begin writing. Don't stop until your allotted time is up.

Schedule #4: The Blitz Writer

The Blitz writer schedules time to write for long periods but less frequently. It's an effective strategy for those who prefer to work in longer, more intense spurts and for those who cannot fit writing into their daily routine. Remember, what you're striving for is to use the most logical, available time you have to maximum advantage.

Novelist Rhonda Pollero has written more than thirty books. When she began writing she was working full time, so she devoted all of her time on Saturdays to her Burning Desire to Write, something she did for ten years before she got published.

"I had a real job and I took Saturdays," she says. "My husband would do all the child care and all that fun stuff, and I literally got to lock myself away in a room one day a week because that was the only time I had."

Now that she makes a living as a writer, Pollero pushes her Blitz writing to new levels. "I'm a very fast writer," she says. "I can do twenty or more pages in a day, but I can't do it seven days a week. So for me, it's budgeting large chunks of time—but not every day." Pollero now uses the Blitz schedule three days out of every week. "I am the person that gets up at one A.M. and tends to write until about three in the afternoon," she says. "Then I'll hang with my family for a while, I'm dead by five thirty, and I'm back up at midnight. I like power writing. I work much better if I plow through."

If you have extraordinary demands on your daily time, experiment with the Blitz schedule. Cumulatively, you can still get in the same amount of time using a Blitz schedule one day a week as you can writing for short amounts of time every day (maybe even more, depending on how many hours you can devote to the Blitz schedule).

Medical suspense writer C.J. Lyons, author of the novel *Arrivals*, is also a Blitz writer, a strategy she adopted while working as a physician. "As a pediatrician I worked part time, which was forty hours a week," she says. "Time to write was obviously scarce, so I would let my stories 'ferment' until I had a day off, and then the words would just flow. It was as if my subconscious would work out all the plot kinks and character problems so that when I actually sat at the computer, I could just pour everything out on to the page."

How to Start Using the Blitz Schedule

Identify at least one day a week that you can devote to writing. Clear your schedule for that one day by blocking out the entire eight hours on your calendar. When that day arrives, you should write that entire time, stopping only for short breaks. Plan ahead so that you will have everything that you need within easy access, such as research notes, paper, printer cartridges, highlighters, food and snacks, coffee or tea, bottled water, pens or pencils, and any other supplies you use when writing. What you *don't* want on that day of Blitz writing is to have to leave your desk, or worse, your home, to go out and get something.

> **"On the commute, you can do a lot of mental work. While you're at work, when you're running the Xerox machine, you can think about your book, and you can be daydreaming while you're sitting at your desk."**
>
> Pamela Morsi, *USA Today* bestselling author

Ideally you can claim an entire eight hours, but if you can only clear your schedule for four hours every Saturday while your family is occupied elsewhere, that's okay. Get as much writing done as you can in that four-hour block of time, but work to gradually increase that over time. The reason you want to have a larger chunk of time is because you're writing less frequently, and you want to use your Blitz schedule to make up for lost time during the week.

I experimented with a Blitz schedule for the first time while writing this book, after I'd interviewed several writers who use it. I set aside some of my winter vacation time and wrote for eight hours a day for four days in a row, stopping twice for thirty minutes to eat and walk. (Remember, I tend to just jump into things. If you decide to use this schedule, start out with one day and build up to more days if you can and want to.) At the end of the four days, I had a draft of the first two-thirds of this book. And I was physically exhausted, mentally drained, and my back ached. Intense periods of sitting and concentrating like that definitely take getting used to. Because I had to return to my full-time job, I resumed my early morning schedule when vacation was over. But because of that one Blitz writing session, I had many pages stacked up in a very short amount of time. I still use a Blitz writing schedule occasionally on weekends, when I want to get a lot of work done in one sitting, or when I need to make up for lost time during the week.

The Blitz schedule works best for aspiring writers whose lifestyle allows them to be away from their obligations for a longer period of time but on a less frequent basis. So if your spouse or a friend can handle your kids all day every Saturday so that you can write, or you can get out of or temporarily delegate other responsibilities, give it a try.

Schedule #5: The Miniblocks-of-Time Writer

Some writers find that a schedule of short, intense writing spurts works best for them. Carving out Miniblocks-of-time is how many writers started their careers. Even a few minutes a day is better than nothing, says novelist Eloisa James. She believes that when you're really under a time crunch, writing for just five minutes is better than nothing, because the worst thing you can face is the empty page. "If you just sit down and say, 'I don't care what it is, I'm going to write it,' then write on that page. Those five minutes, they really build up. They really add on to each other, and before you know it, you have a lot of stuff written," she says.

Writing for a few minutes in the evening is a strategy that Kathryn Lance, the author of more than fifty books of fiction and nonfiction for children and adults, employed as she was learning to balance writing fiction with her other projects and life obligations.

"I used to write a minimum of one fiction sentence every night before going to bed. Or actually, before going to sleep—I did this *in* bed," she says. "I recommend that to people who just can't find time to do their fiction. Often, whatever you are writing takes over and you do several sentences, or paragraphs, or even pages. I wrote most of *Going to See Grassy Ella*, my favorite of my kids' books, that way."

Novelist Beverly Barton found the strategy of working in short increments particularly useful before she was writing for a living. "Years ago, before I sold my first book, I had numerous family obligations and I worked part time," she says, "so I wrote in short intervals—thirty minutes or an hour—whenever I could."

An Egg Timer Supports the Miniblocks-of-Time Schedule

A simple egg timer can be a useful tool for helping you maximize short intervals of time. First, schedule writing in. Then set the timer for the amount of time you want to write, such as ten, twenty, or thirty minutes. This is a trick that Barbara Delinsky, the bestselling author of *Family Tree* and other novels, sometimes uses. "I can write one page in thirty minutes," she says. "If

I'm having trouble sitting here, I set the timer and I refuse to get up until it rings. Sometimes I finish the one page in twenty minutes, and I get up and go get my tea or switch the laundry. I'll set that timer five times in the course of the morning, and by the end, I'm so into it and into the story that I don't need to set it. If you want to do three pages a day, set the timer three times."

How to Start Using the Miniblocks-of-Time Schedule

It's important that you plan ahead and think about where in your day those free minutes or hours already exist. They're there; you just haven't noticed them before. Look at your daily schedule and scrutinize it for those free minutes. This is where your twenty-four-hour time budget can come in handy.

What's already on your schedule that you can frame with some writing time either immediately before or after? Have you identified a fifteen-minute period of time every Tuesday and Thursday that you wait for your chronically late carpool partner to arrive? Do you sit in the car lineup for twenty minutes every afternoon while waiting for your child to be released from school? What about while waiting at doctor's appointments, under the dryer at the hair salon, while getting a pedicure, or waiting for your child's tumbling lessons to end? Maybe it's in the morning while waiting for your coffee to brew, while you wait at your bus stop, or while your toddler naps. For those with employment, consider using the few minutes that you are sitting waiting for staff meetings to begin, or during breaks at in-service trainings.

The key to making Miniblocks-of-time work is to first identify them, then schedule them in. Actively look for this time while you're going about your day. You will discover that there are blocks of time that you weren't previously aware of that you can use for writing. Be on the lookout for these pockets of time and blend writing into them.

Scheduling yourself to working in Miniblocks-of-time is an excellent strategy for incorporating writing into an already time-crunched schedule. Penciling it into your day forms the habit of writing, it makes writing one of your must-do tasks, and following through with your schedule fosters self-discipline. Mini-blocks-of-time can also serve as a motivator to write, because if you know that all you have to do is write for fifteen minutes, then getting to your desk or pulling out your notebook and writing for that small chunk of time feels less daunting. It can also spur you to get words on the page because you only have a short amount of time to get something down, so there's no time to dawdle.

Schedule #6: The Commuting Writer

For those who take public transportation or carpool to work, the daily commute is the perfect opportunity to write. It's time that is already in your day, and it's usually obligation free. Novelist Rick Mofina uses his commute time to support the early morning work he's already put in and the weekend work he is planning. "I use the commute to make notes, usually critical notes to myself, so I know where I'm going," he explains. "They come in handy, and I can feel my story advancing with these notes on a Monday through Friday basis."

How to Start Using the Commuting Writer Schedule

Instead of reading the newspaper, talking with your seat mate, or zoning out by the window, take your work in progress with you and write. If your creativity isn't in high gear in the morning, or if you find it difficult to concentrate in a vehicle full of chatty commuters, try using the time for activities that support your writing:

- Print out pages of your work in progress and review or edit them.
- Jot down plot points for a novel or short story.
- Draft an article or organize your research.
- Brainstorm ideas.
- Write a poem.
- Create character composites by making notes of other commuters' clothing, hairstyles, and snippets of conversation.
- Organize a database of agents, editors, or magazine markets to submit your work to.

The daily commute is the perfect opportunity to get in time to write, especially when you work and commute on a regular basis. The habit is practically built-in to your day. The space holder is already there, it's available, and it's unscheduled time that is an established and natural part of your routine.

Schedule #7: The Any-Opportunity or Combo Writer

Many people are so busy that they have to seize any opportunity to write that is thrown their way. These writers often use a combination of schedules to fit writing into their lives. Bestselling author of *Vanish* and *The Surgeon*, Tess Gerritsen, worked as a physician and wrote for three years before she got her first novel published. She wrote whenever she wasn't on duty. "I would write on my lunch break, as well as after I got home," she says.

"I'd write whenever I could—weekends, early mornings, and late nights. After I got home, as soon as the kids were put down for the night, I'd start writing."

Bestselling author of *Compulsion*, Hilary Norman, used the Any-Opportunity schedule to fit writing into her lifestyle when she was still employed at the BBC. Since that job took more than forty hours a week, she says that when she started writing she had to use all the free time she had to write. "My 'real' work was more than full-time—often working in recording studios on weekends," she says, "so I wrote most evenings and on free weekends."

Some authors alternate strategies as their lifestyles and jobs change, and they adopt a flexible approach to their writing schedule. "I've had a variety of jobs, from teaching college courses, teaching computers, Web developer/programmer to working in bookstores," says Sherrilyn Kenyon (who also writes as Kinley MacGregor), bestselling author of *Devil May Cry*. "While teaching, I wasn't in the classroom every day so I had at least one day a week where I could write undisturbed. While being a programmer, I'd often write instead of eating lunch. With all of them, I stayed up a lot later than I should every night, writing."

Any-Opportunity writers pounce on available time whenever it presents itself. "I find that you just have to get over the hump of thinking you need to sit down and write nonstop until you finish the book," says Arianna Hart, author of *Devil's Playground* and other novels. "You need to really say, 'Okay, I've got two hours here, I'm going to see what I can get done in these two hours.'"

Any-Opportunity writers often double up writing with other duties. "Like most women juggling home, families, and careers,

I multitasked for years before the term became cool," says novelist JoAnn Ross. "I wrote my first completed novel in an Allstate booth in a Phoenix Sears store, once edited a manuscript in the stands at a Rose Bowl game during halftime, and two years ago wrote a scene while sitting in the dentist's chair while waiting for the Novocain to kick in before a root canal."

How to Use the Any-Opportunity Writer Schedule

If you're planning on using the Any-Opportunity or Combo schedule, carry your work in progress with you at all times to take advantage of unexpected free time. Be prepared to write whenever those available moments appear. You should also plan ahead as much as possible. If a block of time opens up suddenly later in the week that you hadn't expected, mark it immediately as time to write. If an appointment cancels, use that hour to write. If you finish chores quicker than you thought you would on the weekend, spend the extra time writing. Be aware of when the time to write presents itself to you and take advantage of it. Even if it's only fifteen minutes here and there, those fifteen minutes add up to a lot of writing at the end of the week.

Accomplished authors have created a variety of schedules that allow them to make time to write no matter what their daily circumstances may be. These schedules work. This is how you find time to write.

chapter five

From No Pages to a Stack of Pages: How You Get There

*a*s outlined in the previous chapter, there is always time to write, you just have to know where to find it. Once you've found that time, you need to create a schedule that fits those opportunities, as well as your personal needs, so that writing becomes a good habit.

The next step is planning how you will spend your writing time so that every single opportunity, no matter how brief, is maximized to the fullest possible extent. You do that by setting goals.

In this chapter, successful writers like Cherry Adair and Hallie Ephron discuss the strategy of goal setting and how it allows them to maximize their productivity while also making writing time highly rewarding. Using these strategies, your writing time will not only fulfill your Burning Desire to Write, but it will be fruitful too.

Why You Need Writing Goals

The reason you need writing goals is simple: they provide the motivation to find time to write. They do this by rewarding you for your accomplishment on a regular basis. It feels good to make progress toward goals, especially in the early days, before you have a readership of fans or a stack of magazines containing your published articles to spur you on to greater success. With a goal system in place, you can measure progress toward your Vision of Success and then feel good about yourself as you watch the pages stack up.

Simply put, a goal is the end result that motivates the behavior necessary to achieve it. All human behavior is goal directed, whether that goal is conscious or not.

Consider this example: you live in a two-story house and your bedroom is upstairs. It's late, cold, and you're tired. Between you and that warm bed—your goal—is a set of stairs. You know you have to climb them, one at a time, to reach that bed.

Falling asleep in the bed represents your Vision of Success. Actually climbing the stair steps to reach the bed represents the specific activities you must accomplish to get you there.

The reason you view it this way is because you want the task of reaching the bed to feel manageable. You can't just leap to the top of the stairs from the ground floor. That's overwhelming. But when you take it step-by-step, you will reach the top of the stairs. So even though you're tired, you still climb those steps because you have a Burning Desire for the end result, which is falling into bed. In the same way, you climb the steps of your writing aspirations, one by one, to reach your Vision of Success.

It's the same concept with writing goals. When you define what you want the end result of your individual and collective writing sessions to be, it makes the activities associated with reaching that ambition clear in your mind. It gives you direction. You have a specific end in mind: your Vision of Success. In order to reach that end, there are specific tasks you must do to get there. Your schedule says that you've got to write for one hour today, so you get it done because it gets you where you want to go.

Goals allow you to maximize even the shortest writing period, because when you sit down, you know the steps you have to take; you know what's at the top of the stairs. Goals help you produce something tangible—words or pages—within your allotted time to write.

Professional Writers Set Goals

Professional writers are successful because they know where they are going before they get started. Cherry Adair, the bestselling author of *White Heat* and *Hot Ice,* built a staircase to her Vision of Success prior to becoming published, and she credits this plan for getting her where she is today. "I wrote a five- and one-year plan," she says. "I stated my goals, then listed the strategies to achieve those goals. Every November I update my career plan. I couldn't have made it this far without it."

Adair's career blueprint is a good example of the type of Writing Action Plan I'm going to teach you to use. There are three components to this plan: long-term goals, short-term-quota goals, and mini-objectives. These are the steps to success for writers in every genre. The three of them work together to make up a solid Writing Action Plan.

Bruce W. Most is a freelancer and author of *Bonded for Murder*. Notice how he breaks his goals down into manageable pieces. "I set goals—for the day, the week, the month, even the year," he says. "For example, I generally have two to three hours to write fiction a day. If I'm writing a draft, I try to average a minimum number of written words during that time. Sometimes I don't make it, sometimes I do better, depending on how a particular chapter is going. But the word goal gives me something to strive for, pushes me along."

In Most's example, his yearly goal represents his long-term goal. It's the top of the staircase for him. His monthly, weekly, and daily goals are the steps of that staircase—in other words, these are his short-term-quota goals and mini-objectives.

The SMART Way to Set Goals

Goals give your writing direction and provide you with the means to get to your Vision of Success. So how do you create effective goals?

When I first began work as a counselor, I was taught to help people set goals using the SMART acronym:

- **S=Specific.** Goals define in detail the outcome you are striving to reach.
- **M=Measurable.** A measurable goal is one that allows you to track your progress along the way. It states how much or how many of something you'll produce.
- **A=Achievable.** Set goals that you know you can accomplish. This is a subjective task. A good rule of thumb is if you consistently meet your goals quickly and easily, they aren't high enough and you should adjust them.

- **R=Realistic.** Set yourself up for success by setting goals that will challenge you yet that you know you can accomplish. Remember that creative high achievers set moderately difficult goals. People who set goals crave that feeling of accomplishment. However, if goals are so lofty that they're unattainable, people get discouraged and give up. So you don't want your first goal to be "Write a Pulitzer Prize–winning novel." A better goal is "Write a novel."
- **T=Time Limited.** All goals have a target date for completion. Long-term goals can cover twelve months to twenty years, but I recommend you keep them to twelve months for manageability purposes. Short-term-quota goals cover a period of up to six months and as little as thirty days. Mini-objectives are quick action steps that can be accomplished in as little as one to ten days.

Example of Long-Term Goal

Long-term goals are broad, overarching statements of what you want to accomplish in twelve months. An example of a long-term goal is, "I will write a novel within twelve months," or "I will become a freelance writer within one year," or "I'll write five short stories by the end of the year." Long-term goals are a one-line reflection of your Vision of Success. They are the top of your staircase.

Example of Short-Term-Quota Goal

Short-term-quota goals are the steps of the staircase. They cover one to six months. What makes quota goals so useful for writers is that they contain a number that you use as an indicator of progress. Think of a quota as a measuring stick—it states how much or how many of something you'll produce that moves you toward achievement of your long-term goal. Examples include setting a certain number of words or pages you'll write every day. This makes it very easy for you to measure your progress because you can count it.

> **"If I write fifteen pages in a day, I consider that good."**
>
> Beverly Barton, *New York Times* bestselling author

Say your long-term goal is, "I will write a novel within twelve months." Now you need to state what you'll do over the next one to six months to get that novel written. If you've chosen the Early-Morning schedule, your quota goal might be: "I will write *five hundred* words of my novel every morning for the next six months." If you've chosen the Blitz schedule, your quota goal might be, "I will write *three pages* of my novel every week for the next thirty days." See? There's a number of words or pages there that you can count. Those numbers help you to know, on a day-to-day basis, how much progress you're making toward your long-term goal of writing a novel.

Quota goals are influenced by the genre you write in. For instance, if you're aiming to get a three-thousand-word essay written to submit to an anthology, and you're writing for thirty minutes in the evening after your kids are in bed, your short-term-quota goal might be to write one hundred words per day for thirty days. If you're writing a novel, which is longer and more involved, and you're using the Miniblocks-of-time schedule, your quota goal might be to write a half page per day.

Notice how both goals follow the SMART format: they are specific (the products will be a novel, five hundred words, or three pages respectively), measurable (you will know you've achieved the goals if you have a novel, your five hundred words, or your three pages), achievable and realistic (again, set your goals according to what you can do), and time limited (twelve months, six months, and one month.)

These goals are also influenced by your chosen writing schedule. Since you want to set achievable and realistic goals to start out with, if you're not hitting your quota goals at least somewhat regularly, you need to examine why. Are you ignoring your schedule? Maybe the schedule you set isn't the ideal one for you. Say you're using the After-Hours schedule and had planned to write from nine to eleven P.M., but you're getting sidelined by *The David Letterman Show*, your kids' school projects, or late-night housekeeping duties.

Use your quota goal to assess this problem. If you wanted to write two pages every night and you just aren't doing it consistently, you need to look at correcting what is interfering with that or, if that isn't possible, using a different schedule. You can also adjust your quota.

A Page-Quota Goal

A page-quota goal, where you set a certain number of pages that you will write at each session, is an effective tool for those who want to put the emphasis less on time and more on getting a specific amount of work produced during their writing appointment. Some writers get deep satisfaction from creating a small stack of pages each time they write, even if it's just two or three sheets.

A page quota can help you keep yourself in the chair, because you know if you've got to get to a certain number of pages, then you don't get up until that's accomplished. You also need a schedule that can accommodate longer periods of writing time, because for page quotas to work, you have to allow for more writing time on days when you need to make up for times when the words didn't flow as well.

A page quota is the measuring stick that Rebecca York (the pen name of Ruth Glick), bestselling author of *New Moon* and other novels, uses for getting her writing done. "I write a certain number of pages every day," she says, "usually ten. I stay at the computer and work until I get those pages done."

A page quota is a useful indicator for measuring progress toward getting a large project, such as a book, finished. Novelist Robyn Carr uses a page-quota goal that reflects her long-term goal of getting a draft completed in a set amount of time. "At five pages a day, I can have a first draft of a novel in three months," she says.

Page quotas are good for writers because they can be adapted to fit your lifestyle. For example, novelist Carly Phillips's quota goal is to write twenty-five pages per week in a five-day work week, but sometimes the amount in a single day isn't up to par.

Instead of just abandoning her goal of writing five pages a day, she tallies up her work at the end of the week. It's the *weekly* page quota that keeps her on track with her writing. "For me, that's five pages a day, five days a week," she says. "Or two pages one day and seven the next. I don't much care how I tally the pages, as long as those pages get written. And I admit, when the weekend rolls around, if I'm running short on page count, I'm working a lot harder to make those pages up." This is an excellent example of how quotas can support and even boost your writing output.

Notice that this is also how Phillips holds herself accountable. That's the beauty of short-term-quota goals. They allow you to track your progress on a regular basis and assess how well you're doing towards reaching your primary, or long-term, goal. With ongoing scrutiny, you either adjust the output number if it doesn't work for you, or you exercise self-discipline to meet your quota goal.

Guidelines for Using the Page Quota

If you choose to use a page quota, set a goal that's attainable for you. "You can't set your writing goals based on your best day of writing," says novelist Kathy Carmichael. "I've twice written forty-two pages in one day. Both times it nearly killed me. I'm not going to set forty-two pages-per-day writing goals!"

Carmichael suggests that instead writers figure out what they can easily and consistently write. She says that if it's one page per day, then that should be your goal. That way you can meet your short-term goal, and if you exceed it you feel great. "So your weekly goal would be five pages," she explains. "If you accomplish that, great, you knew you could. If you write ten pages instead of your goal of five, you've done awesome." As your skills improve, you can also increase the number of pages you aim to write at each session, if you so choose.

Again, notice the flexibility balanced with holding oneself accountable. Carmichael has set her page quota at a level that causes her to challenge herself but that can also be achieved consistently. And she often exceeds that goal and writes more. Either way, it is rewarding, and it gets the writing done.

Mary Jo Putney, the bestselling author of *The Marriage Spell*, is another successful writer who uses a page quota. She says that when she's in working mode, she usually writes every day. But she takes a flexible approach to her page quota and balances achievement with lifestyle needs. "Ideally, if I can do four pages a day, I feel pretty good about it; I feel like I'm in a good flow," she says. This is one reason many writers use page quotas: a feeling of accomplishment.

Other writers find that using page quotas even enhances the creative process. Novelist Eloisa James uncovered this hidden benefit to the practice of writing twenty pages in one sitting. "What happens is the first ten are hard and you're completely exhausted, and then the second ten will go much faster," she says. "And they'll be much more imaginative and much more free. What I generally discover is that in later days, I often have to cut the first ten, but that second ten will be really good."

Remember that page-quota goals, like all goals, should be challenging but not overwhelming. Select a page quota that you can consistently achieve. If you miscalculate how many pages your writing style can produce in a day or week, you can simply make adjustments. "The page goal should be reasonable, but should also be ambitious," says Vicki Lewis Thompson, author of *My Nerdy Valentine* and other novels.

To determine if a page-quota strategy is right for you, set a number of pages per day or week that you feel you can accomplish, and stick with it for thirty days. If it's too hard, drop back the number. If it's too easy, increase it. Strive to reach a middle-of-the-road number that is rewarding and makes your writing time productive.

A Word-Quota Goal

Another quota is the word quota. This involves defining a predetermined number of words to be written in a given session.

Novelist Steve Berry gives an example of how he does it. "I like to do five hundred to one thousand words a day," he says.

"I go until my brain says, 'I've had enough for today, I'm tired.' Some days I can do two thousand words, some days no. Five hundred to one thousand words is a good goal for me, which is about two to four pages. If I can do those, fine."

Notice how Berry gives himself some latitude with the quota and has a range that he aims for each day. Since the creative process ebbs and flows, it's okay to give yourself some wiggle room. Just like with a page quota, you can make up the word count later in the week when the words are flowing better for you.

Like page quotas, word quotas are a useful tool that help you reach your long-term goals by breaking down the total required output into a manageable amount. A word quota is a valuable aide for organizing projects, especially larger ones like a novel, into small, doable pieces. Word quotas give you a concrete number of words that you must get on the page at each writing session. This way you can easily monitor your progress, plan your work, and adjust your output as needed. For example, award-winning writer Hallie Ephron, coauthor of the Dr. Peter Zak mystery series, uses a word quota; it's her measuring stick of choice because she knows she can produce a book that way in a set amount of time. "I set myself a five-hundred-word-a-day goal," she says. "That's not very much, that's a page-and-a-half double spaced. But if I can do that, I can finish a first draft in six months."

As with page quotas, set a word quota that is achievable but realistic for you. Work it for thirty days and then adjust if necessary.

A Time-Quota Goal

The third type of quota is spending a specified amount of time at the writing desk. Some writers use their schedule as their quota goal. That's fine. If it's easier for you to say that you'll be at your desk for one hour every morning, and that's your short-term-quota goal, no problem. You can count up the minutes, and it's a good way to reinforce a new writing schedule.

A time quota is useful for those who like to stop and process their writing while they're doing it. So within the one-hour allotted writing time, you may not actually write for that entire period, but you are actively present with the work in progress. You may commit to getting a scene of your novel down and then spend time considering various plot points, revising earlier work, or doing research.

Daphne Kalotay, the author of *Calamity and Other Stories,* uses a time quota and takes this less formulaic approach to the strategy. "I know that if I'm having a good writing day I can keep it up for about four hours," she says. "After that my brain pretty much shuts off. So if I have a block of time, I try to sit at my desk for around four hours total, even if nothing's 'happening' for part of that time."

This is a good approach. You may commit to writing as much as you can for at least thirty minutes without stopping, and then spend the rest of the time revising, editing, or working on plot line. The key is that the writing schedule is already in place, and you want to capitalize on it.

The nice thing about a time quota, especially for beginners, is that you are training yourself to show up at your desk consistently. If you sit there long enough, something is bound to happen.

This is a strategy that Ann Major, the bestselling author of *The Secret Lives of Doctors' Wives*, uses. Again, note the flexibility balanced with achievement. "This afternoon, I'm only going to write from two to four thirty," she says. "I'm going to sit there and I'm really going to try to write five pages in that two-and-a-half hours, and if I do that, it'll be fabulous."

Novelist Eloisa James believes that a time quota is especially valuable for beginning writers, since it may help improve the quality of what gets written. She suggests that if you're using a word quota, you're focused on how many words you've put down on the page rather than the quality of the writing. "One thing that a lot of beginning writers do that marks an early manuscript, and generally a poor one, is they write way too much exposition," she explains. If you're trying for a word count, you write a lot of words, and "a part of you isn't going to want to delete because you've got this word count to get to. Whereas with a time quota, the only thing you're saying is, 'Between four and five, I'm going to sit there and write.'"

Time quotas also support the creative process. Renee Bernard, author of *A Lady's Pleasure*, says time quotas are useful because they compensate for less productive days. "I find when I set page goals I feel myself powering down. *I've written eleven pages and I was going to write ten, okay I get to quit.* If I was on a roll, I want to keep going. So I set time goals, and then if I'm on a roll, I keep going and ride that wave as long as I can to compensate for the days when I absolutely do not feel like [writing]," she says.

If your writing schedule is one hour every Saturday morning, your time quota is to simply sit and write whatever comes to you during that time. It may be one thousand words, it may be ten. Focus on the amount of time you're at your desk versus how many words or pages you've gotten done.

Time quotas also help you reach your long-term goals. If you know that you can usually write one page every thirty minutes, then you can plan out how many hours you'll need to be at your desk each week in order to reach your long-term goal by the target date.

Nonfiction Writers Use Query Quotas

A different type of quota is used by writers who target periodicals for their work. Aspiring to write for magazines presents a unique challenge because you don't write your article until after an editor accepts the idea. So rather than sitting down to write the actual article, you write a query instead.

This is how a query quota works: nonfiction writers assign themselves the task of writing and mailing out a set number of queries per day, week, or month, pitching ideas to editors of magazines and journals. It's a practice that they start and often continue for the duration of their careers.

Karen Asp, a freelance writer who specializes in fitness, utilized query quotas when she was working to establish herself as a writer. The strategy worked so well that she continues the practice to this day. "I had to send out three new queries a week," she says, "and that's still my goal. That has stuck ever since I started freelancing in 1999."

Freelancer Sandra J. Gordon used a query quota, but she approached the process in a slightly different manner. "I used to have sixteen to twenty queries out at a time, five ideas to twenty different magazines," she says. "I wouldn't put out queries daily, I'd do it every two weeks. I'd query a lot, and then I'd rest."

Gordon adds that she was careful not to send twenty queries to the same person, but rather worked to ensure that her material was circulating at a good pace to a selection of editors.

When setting a query quota, aim for a number that will challenge you but that you think is reasonable to obtain. Drafting a solid query usually requires research and sometimes interviewing sources. For example, if you want to write an article on the latest treatments for carpal tunnel syndrome, you will have to research the problem and probably call an expert to gather more information. It takes time to locate that source and set up the interview, talk to the person, transcribe your notes, and then draft the query letter. All of that counts as writing time.

> "Finding a system that worked for me was the ultimate light bulb moment. No two writers approach the process the same way, nor should they."
>
> Rhonda Pollero, *USA Today* bestselling author

You also have to identify markets to send the query to and locate the appropriate editor's name and address. You have to check the magazine's guidelines to find out if they take e-mail queries or snail mail queries. If they only accept snail mail queries, that requires extra time for printing out a clean copy of the query, creating address labels, and getting the envelope ready to mail.

If you only have two hours a day designated as writing time, some of that time will have to be used for all those additional activities. So play with your query quota to determine how much time it takes to actually get your queries written and mailed out. You might be able to send out three queries a week, like Asp, or maybe your creativity lists more toward Gordon's Blitz style.

After you start landing assignments, you may have to adjust the quota based on the amount of time the article will take to write along with balancing your other responsibilities and continuing to send out queries. If you only write for two hours in the morning before leaving for work, you won't be able to put out ten queries a month if you get an assignment to write an article for *National Geographic* magazine, because you'll probably have to use that time to write your article instead. So get your article done on time, and then get right back to your query quota.

The query quota system motivates periodical writers to find time to write by rewarding them for meeting output goals and then by selling the articles their queries reference. It demonstrates that no matter how complex your writing needs are, there are effective strategies to make time to write and boost productivity.

Mini-Objectives

Mini-objectives are the last piece of the writing action plan. Like goals, they are specific, measurable, achievable, realistic, and time limited. Think of them as your daily writing to-do list. Mini-objectives can be accomplished in a day, a week, or two weeks. Sometimes they're a one-time action step. You can have as many or as few as necessary to support reaching your goals. The best part is that you get to frequently check them off as completed!

Some examples of mini-objectives are:

- Start using the Early-Morning writer schedule and set the alarm clock back in five-minute increments beginning tomorrow. Continue for ten days until I'm getting up one hour earlier to write.

- Make a list by tomorrow of the chores that need to be accomplished every evening so I can begin writing by seven p.m.
- Talk to spouse tonight about picking up the kids from school two days a week so that I can write during that time.
- Put notebook and extra pens in purse/briefcase tonight so that I can make notes about my novel during carpool time.
- Go to the library for an hour every day after work this week and do research on carpal tunnel syndrome.
- Check out a book this weekend on how to write query letters.

Notice how the mini-action goals are very specific and easily accomplished. You focus on them briefly, check them off, and then move on. That's what you're striving for: quick, doable, highly detailed steps that zip you along toward your long-term goal.

chapter six

Your Writing Action Plan

*L*ong-term goals, short-term-quota goals, and mini-objectives work together to create a personal and results-oriented Writing Action Plan. The first step, as mentioned before, is to choose the writing schedule you'll use. Next, create goals that you believe you can accomplish using that schedule. In this chapter, I'll give you two examples of a Writing Action Plan, and then I'd like you to create your own plan using the blank template that follows.

Sample Fiction Writing Action Plan Using the Early Morning Schedule

Long-Term Goal: *I will write a novel.* Target date for completion: *March 15* (twelve months from today)

Short-Term-Quota Goal: *I will write two pages of my novel every weekday for the next six months.* Target date for completion: *September 15* (six months from today)

Mini-objective One: *Beginning tomorrow, set alarm clock back in five-minute increments until I am rising at four thirty A.M. to write every day before work.* Target date for completion: *March 25* (ten days from today)

Mini-objective Two: *Create a detailed outline with plot points for my novel.* Target date for completion: *March 31* (two weeks from today)

Are these goals:
Specific? *Yes. In the long-term goal, I'm giving myself twelve months to produce a novel. In the short-term-quota goal, I'm setting a specific page amount (two) to write over the next six months. In the mini-objectives, I'm giving myself specific short-term actions to take on a daily basis.*

Measurable? *Yes. At the end of twelve months, I'll know if I've met my long-term goal if I have a draft of a novel. I can count how many pages I write every weekday, and it should be two. I should also be getting up at four thirty by the end of ten days, and I should have an outline with plot points by the end of two weeks.*

Achievable and realistic? *Yes, for me.*

Time limited? *Yes. They all have a specific target date for completion. At the end of six months, I'll reassess my short-term-quota goal* *and update it for the next six months; if it's working, I'll continue it, if it's not, I'll adjust it.*

Sample Nonfiction Writer Using After-Hours Schedule

Long-Term Goal: I will get published in two national magazines. Target date for completion: January 1 (twelve months from today)

Short-Term-Quota Goal: *I will send out one magazine query per month.* Target date for completion: *June 1* (six months from today)

Mini-objective One: *Go to the library after work and study the magazines I want to get published in.* Target date for completion: *January 5* (five days from today)

Mini-objective Two: *Identify six topics that I could write about that are appropriate to those magazines.* Target date for completion: *January 7* (seven days from today)

Mini-objective Three: *Locate an expert in my chosen topic and schedule an interview with that person.* Target date for completion: *January 10* (ten days from today)

These goals also follow the SMART format: *specific (get published in two magazines, send out one query per month, go to the library for one week), measurable (two magazines, one query, identify six topics, schedule an interview), achievable and realistic (for me), and time limited (twelve months, six months, five days, ten days.)*

Your Writing Action Plan

Now it's your turn. Use the template below to create your own Writing Action Plan. Remember to use the SMART format, and make sure you include the actual date for reaching each one:

Writing Action Plan

Long-Term Goal: _____

_____

_____

                     TARGET DATE: _____

Short-Term-Quota Goal: _____

_____

_____

                     TARGET DATE: _____

Mini-objective ONE: _____

_____

_____

                     TARGET DATE: _____

Mini-objective TWO: _____

_____

_____

                     TARGET DATE: _____

Mini-objective THREE: _____

_____

_____

                     TARGET DATE: _____

Do your goals follow the SMART format?

Specific? How? _____

_____

Measurable? How? _____

_____

Achievable for you? How? _____

_____

Realistic for you? How? _____

_____

Time limited? How? _____

_____

Hold Yourself Accountable by Tracking Your Progress

An important component to success in meeting goals is to develop a way to hold yourself accountable for meeting them. You need to track your progress, or lack thereof, toward those goals. Here is where many people get off track. They have a goal but they have no way of knowing if they're making progress toward it. Devising a tracking mechanism is a critical element. The easiest way to do this is to make a checklist that lets you mark off when you met your goals for that week.

Novelist Carly Phillips gives an example of how she monitors her daily strides. "In a binder, I print and put blank Goal Sheets, broken down by week—one page per week and divided by days," she says. "The top of each page/week has the page I'm supposed to be on when the week ends. It's an effective means of keeping me on my toes, and every day I jot down page count—what I wrote, or didn't write, and why. I make myself accountable."

Develop a similar tracking system for your own goals. Don't make it hard. Just create a form on your computer or put pages in a binder like Phillips does and mark off if you did or did not meet your quota goal for that day. Tally the numbers and make them up at the end of the week if you need to. It can also be helpful to note why you did or did not meet your goal, as Phillips does, to help tweak your goal setting in the future.

It's a psychological fact that whenever you start counting the number of times a certain behavior occurs, that behavior will temporarily increase or decrease, depending on whichever one you want it to do. That's because you're bringing the habit, or lack of it, into your everyday, routine awareness.

If one of your goals is to write five hundred words every day, and you check off whether or not you did that, you're bringing the concept of "write five hundred words every day" into your daily, routine awareness. The habit of writing five hundred words every day will increase immediately because you want to make that little check on your sheet. Try it. It's easy, it's simple, and it works.

It's a good idea to tape your Writing Action Plan somewhere that you will see it often: next to your computer, on the bathroom mirror, on the cabinet above your coffeemaker. Write the target dates for completion in your calendar in red ink. Read your plan aloud every morning. Doing these things is another way to reinforce the habit of writing and to hold yourself accountable to your plan.

Setting writing goals will put you miles down the road in terms of becoming a successful writer, and you'll routinely be fulfilling your Burning Desire to Write.

chapter seven

How to Create Time to Write

Finding time to begin a writing career is similar to starting any other enterprise from which you hope to one day earn your living or beginning any new activity that you previously have not had time for—going to a gym every day, for example. It will take time to adjust. It may require rearranging or sacrificing other activities in order to establish your new routine.

In this chapter, we'll hear from successful authors such as Wendy Corsi Staub and Jennifer Blake on how they manage the sacrifices inherent in becoming a successful writer and the rewards they reap by fulfilling their Burning Desire to Write.

When it comes to writing, your middle-level needs on Maslow's hierarchy—your social activities—may have to take low priority for a while as you tend to your writing goals. The time to write must come from somewhere, and since you've made it one of your must-do activities, time spent in other hobbies or leisure interests will naturally take lower priority than writing, at least in the beginning while you're working to get established.

Successful writers understand this. They know that time to write isn't something you *have*, it's something you *create*. It can be created by giving up something else, such as sleeping in on the weekends. But over time the balance rights itself, and activities that were initially sacrificed can be enjoyed again if desired.

A Matter of Perspective

Sacrificing some things you enjoy in order to get in your writing doesn't have to be an agonizing experience. Look back at your twenty-four-hour time budget and decide how much time you are spending in activities that aren't meaningful to you and don't fulfill you. It's likely that there are several places within your day that you're doing something that wouldn't hurt too bad to eliminate for writing.

Nobody says you have to give up watching *Dancing with the Stars* if you simply must see it, but in order to fit writing into your busy life, it's critical that you decide what's important to you and what's not. You have to set priorities. What's leisure time and what's just slacking off time? *Dancing with the Stars* is a sixty-minute show. Are you getting sucked into watching whatever comes on after it, even though you aren't really interested in it? There's where you can write instead, or go to bed so that you can get up early the next day to write. Do you only care about who is getting voted off, which happens in the last ten minutes? Write up until that happens and then again afterwards. Obviously, there are some things that you can't—and shouldn't—give up for writing: time spent meeting the needs of your children, spouse, or partner, your own self-care routines, going to your job, exercising, caring for pets or elderly family members, basic housekeeping chores, and so forth. But you can achieve a balance. As some professional writers have already demonstrated, you can write while doing other activities, for instance, while watching your children's ballgames. You can also write while your kids are doing their homework, while your spouse is napping on Saturday afternoon, or when you take breaks from cleaning house. Perhaps an older child can set the table before dinner so that you can write. If yard maintenance is taking up a lot of your time, try hiring the kid up the street to cut the grass to relieve you of that obligation.

> "I went to college and studied writing in Boston, and the teacher said that some people have real talent. And then there's the rest of us, and the rest of us just work. It's in our blood. We may not be the best writers in the world, but we get it done. And that's 50 percent of writing."
>
> Jennifer Quasha, freelance writer and book author

Other things may be okay to give up totally until or even after you get your writing schedule firmly in place—your weekly facial at the spa, perhaps, or watching old game highlights on ESPN. Maybe that's the only time you have to write, and so you choose to give that up because that needs to be your hour of scheduled writing time now.

If preparing dinner is taking up too much time in the evening, can you purchase more prepared deli food, or cook meals ahead of time on Sunday and heat them up throughout the week?

Look at your day and determine what discretionary tasks are consuming too much of your time, then create a plan for giving them up, shifting them to other time spots, or using them as rewards for getting your writing done.

This is one way to accommodate your family's lifestyle to your writing schedule. As you consistently work on your schedule, and writing becomes a habit, your family will adjust also. They'll learn that Mom-or-Dad-the-aspiring-writer isn't available from six to seven every night because he or she is writing.

Writing Is a Choice

The truth is most writers don't mind giving up some television, getting up a little earlier on Saturday, or skipping lunch with coworkers so that they can write—because they love to write! Writers want to write. It's a choice; one they happily make. Yes, it may be hard to sit inside and churn out those three pages of your novel on a beautiful Saturday afternoon, but when you get your novel finished, won't it be worth it? Of course it will.

And as your writing output increases and you meet your quota goals, you may be able to readjust your schedule and write during a time when it doesn't feel like such a sacrifice. Or, as happened with me, you may simply get used to writing during a specific time. Writing becomes a habit, and that is the real strength of adhering to a schedule.

Most writers choose to write over most other activities because they want to. Again, this is their Burning Desire; it stills the restlessness they feel inside when they aren't writing, and it helps them to feel self-actualized, which is at the very top of Maslow's hierarchy of needs. Remember that self-actualization is the pinnacle of individual achievement and fulfillment.

When You're Caught Between a Rock and a Hard Place

Since the idea of giving up some things you enjoy in order to make time to write may seem discouraging, consider this metaphor: A man had rocks of various sizes that he was attempting to fit into a jar. First he placed all of the small rocks in the jar, but the large rocks would not fit in around them. But by putting the large rocks in first, he discovered that the small rocks slipped into place around them, and the jar could easily hold everything.

What this metaphor teaches us is this: do the important activities first and the others will fall into place around it. Make time to write one of your big rocks. In other words, in the beginning of your writing career, when you're still a wet-behind-the-ears newbie, you will likely have to give up something in order to make time to write. If you rise early to write before your job, you'll have to sacrifice sleep. If you choose to write on the weekends, you'll have to sacrifice your leisure time, and so forth. The trick is to get your writing done first whenever possible, and everything else will fall into place around it.

Reward Yourself for Writing

Rewarding yourself for writing is the key to managing sacrifice. Many writers reward themselves with the very activities they gave up. They allow themselves an hour of television, gardening, or napping in exchange for an hour of writing.

The ability to balance writing with leisure time is a natural byproduct of goal setting and keeping your eye trained on success. When becoming a successful writer is your long-term goal, giving up some fun stuff is tolerable because you know it will pay off eventually. Giving up pleasurable activities is not necessarily a permanent situation. "It's about time management and prioritizing," says novelist Kathy Carmichael. "Narrowing my focus down to those things I really want or need to do versus those things I'm willing to give up, even for a short time, is what works for me."

Carmichael makes a critical point here: what are you willing to give up, even for a short time, in order to write? Finding time to write is not an all or nothing, black or white situation. Look at your twenty-four-hour time budget and decide what discretionary or non-obligation tasks you can give up for a short time in order to accomplish writing.

> **"I make deals with myself. If I work for such and such a time, or I do so many pages, I'm allowed to play a video game, or shop, or go to the casino, or take a nap, or whatever else it is that I think I want to do."**
>
> Tara Taylor Quinn, *USA Today* bestselling author

Sacrificing leisure time in order to make time to write is a common theme among professional writers. Jennifer Blake, the bestselling author of *Rogue's Salute* and other novels, believes there's a unique payoff to making these sacrifices because she's a writer. She says she's given up "good times—times that could have been spent enjoying family and friends, lying in the sun, walking in the rain." But Blake feels that when she is able to participate in these activities, she appreciates them all the more. In other words, the rewards are greater because she's a writer. "The fact that I write makes the hours spent actually doing these things matter more," she says, "because I'm more acutely aware, more present in the moment."

When becoming a successful writer is your long-term goal, reaching that goal is the ultimate reward. Becoming a successful novelist is so important to Wendy Corsi Staub, bestselling author of *Don't Scream* and other novels, that she has chosen to give up many of her hobbies in order to make time to write. "The past two years have been so demanding that I've now pretty much given up all pleasure reading, crafts, television programs, gardening, time with friends, my gym membership," she says, "and many, many hours of sleep."

But it's been worth it. The payoff for Staub is the fact that she's now living her dream. "I've wanted to be an author since I was eight, and now I'm living my dream career!" she says. "I can't think of anything more positive than that. No matter how exhausting and overwhelming my deadlines are, I honestly wake up every morning feeling like the luckiest girl in the world and counting my blessings."

Initially, making the decision to write instead of engaging in a hobby or joining friends for a long lunch on a Saturday afternoon nurtures the mindset that writing is a priority, which will empower you to move forward in your journey. Remember: successful writers write no matter what. You've got to take consistent action toward your dream. Freelance writer and editor Tim O'Shei, who began his writing career while he was holding down a full-time job as a teacher, says that writing when he could have been playing didn't allow him much time for a life. He made the decision and stuck with it because becoming a writer was his dream, and he loves it. "The people you get to meet are fascinating," he says, "and the impact that you can have as a writer, it goes beyond what you'll ever know."

Rewards mount as success is earned. As you work your schedule, your skills improve and you become a better writer. You make visible progress toward your long-term goals. This leads to a positive association with writing, and you enjoy doing it. The payoff begins to show, and so you seek writing out. "Yesterday I got asked to do something that I really wanted to," says Merline Lovelace, bestselling author *Ex Marks the Spot* and other novels, "but I said, 'Sorry I can't do it.'"

The payoff, of course, is that Lovelace gets to set her own schedule. "Being your own boss is wonderful. I just love being able to set my own schedule, work out of my home, and do what I want to do with my life."

Other writers have discovered that sacrificing leads to rewards that may not, at first, be obvious. Nina Foxx, author of *Marrying Up*, found that balancing a social life with her writing time required sacrifice, but the payoff is that she makes a living as a writer and can spend more time with her children. "There's a lot of people who want to go to lunch or go shopping, and I can't," she says. "In this business, if you don't produce you don't get paid, obviously. I have to make myself be very disciplined. But the tradeoff is I can be with my kids. If I need to be a mom in the classroom, I can do that. I'm free to travel whenever I want to. It's a great thing."

Turning down fun or desirable activities is something that successful writers frequently do, especially when the writing is going well. "When I'm here and everything's clicking, I work long days," says novelist Sandra Brown. "I don't take off and go shopping, I don't take off and go to lunch with friends, things like that."

Like Lovelace, the payoff for Brown is that she can balance those sacrifices with taking time off when she wants or needs to. "I have very good friends with whom I'll go to Europe after a book is finished," she says. "I do have the luxury of saying the days I'm going to be off. I don't have to check with the boss first."

Time spent with friends or recreational activities will usually be the first to go, simply because that's the most logical and available time you have to trade for your dream. "The biggest sacrifice you will make, if you want to become a successful writer, is you sacrifice your own time. You're not only going to have to sacrifice your time that you spend with loved ones and others, you're going to have to sacrifice time that you want to read a book or see a movie," says bestselling author of *Scandalous Lovers*, Robin Schone. "But you've got to say, 'This is what I've got to do.'"

Deciding that you're going to do what you have to do to become a writer is a critical element for balancing writing and sacrifice, says freelancer Stephanie Losee. "First, you have to decide that you have something to say and that you have to say it," she says. "The second part is you have to say that what one man can do, another can do. Somewhere out there is somebody who is doing twice as much as you are and who has three books to their credit. The third is just decide that you will not be denied, that you want to be a writer. Finally, in the end, decide that you're willing to do things that other people are not willing to do."

Some Writers Don't View It as Sacrifice

Other successful writers, like bestselling novelist Joy Fielding, author of *Mad River Road,* feel that the rewards inherent in working as a professional writer automatically outweigh any sacrifices. For Fielding, writing never detracted from her life, it gave her a life. "I honestly don't think I've given anything up," she says. "For me, writing has always been the perfect thing to do. I never feel like it's a job, I enjoy it so much. It allows me such freedom."

Novelist Barbara Samuel expresses a similar sentiment. "The work is its own reward," she says. "It's so very, very good for me and my life, that anything I had to give up to get it was the right choice."

Other Sacrifices, Other Rewards

Giving up a few hours of television or napping on Saturday isn't the only sacrifice writers make. Another is that of camaraderie and working with others. In Maslow's hierarchy, the middle levels of human need consist of love and a sense of belonging. This can be as part of a family, having central friendships, and seeing office mates daily. As a full-time writer, you do not go into an office with others who are doing the same job as you. There's no one in the next cubicle to bounce problems off of or vent to about management. Professional full-time writers know they must take precautions to balance the isolation that writing brings while ensuring that their middle-level needs continue to be met. "Writing is such a solitary existence," explains novelist Julia London, "and I have, at various points in time, become so engrossed in the book I am writing, I forget to have conversations with real people. Not only is that not good for my writing, it's not good for me."

London successfully offsets this lack of camaraderie by rewarding herself with the very activities she gave up. "In addition to making sure I write every day, I also make sure I do something that is out of my little world every day," she says. Spending time with her husband, exercising, and traveling are ways that London balances the aloneness of a writing career with real life needs.

When choosing the activities that you'll temporarily give up in order to pursue your dream of becoming a working writer, balance your choices by building in interactions with your family, friends, and social groups as a way of keeping your life in perspective. There's no sense in tossing aside all of your leisure activities if it will only serve to depress or demotivate you. The trick to making time to write within the context of your busy life is to weave writing into your existing day. Make writing part of your lifestyle.

Laura Fraser is a freelance writer and author of the bestselling travel memoir *An Italian Affair*. Along with some colleagues, Fraser has taken a unique approach to combating the isolation that working as a professional freelancer can bring. "I have an office outside my home and I go to it every day with regular hours," she says. "I actually work with some other freelancers in a shared office, and that gives us a sense of support and community, which benefits everyone."

Other freelancers balance the sacrifice of camaraderie by focusing on the positives that being an independent writer brings to their lives. "I think one of the biggest sacrifices is not having that group of people you see at work every day," says Elizabeth Shimer, a freelance writer who specializes in health and women's issues. "When I was working full time, I realized that my coworkers were the people I saw more than anyone, and they really do form a special place in your life. Now I don't have that. But I do have the freedom to work when I want to, so it's a tradeoff."

Treating Writing Like a Job Helps to Manage Sacrifices

If you won the lottery, would you quit your job? I think I would. The reason I give up eight hours of my life, five days a week, and go into an office is so that I can have money to keep a roof over my head and food on the table. There are certain lifestyle changes I've made to accommodate my day job. I don't go out on weeknights because I know I have to get up early for work the next day. I coordinate my vacations with my employer's needs for my time. I sacrifice things that are important to me: sleeping late, blowing off work to sit around and watch TV all day, and yes, even writing time, because if I don't go to work, I'll lose my job. But the rewards are the fact that I have a steady paycheck, affordable health insurance, there are aspects of my job that I truly enjoy, and working in the world gives me ideas and perspectives that I can bring to my writing.

This is the mindset you've got to adopt with writing. Even if you don't get paid yet, or paid much, and even if it is not your goal to ever get paid for it, writing is a job that you need to show up at, consistently, in order to reap the rewards of meeting your goals and fulfilling your Burning Desire to Write. This is a key strategy for finding time to write in day-to-day life and managing the sacrifices that go along with that. Treat writing like a job even before it's a paid job.

If you've started working within your writing schedule, you've probably already come to this realization. You go to your desk every day and write a certain amount, just like you go to your paid job every day at a specified time and stay there for a pre-determined amount of time. While at work, you have specific work items and goals that you are expected to accomplish. So give yourself specific tasks (your quota goals) when you sit down to write that you want to accomplish that session. Approaching writing this way is an excellent strategy that can set you up to succeed, but you've got to be a good self-employee. You've got to hold yourself accountable to your schedule and your Writing Action Plan.

There Are Many Benefits to the Writing-Is-a-Job Mindset

The writing-is-a-job mindset serves multiple purposes: since you know that any sacrifices are short term in nature, you're motivated to keep working on your Writing Action Plan. Treating writing like a job also fosters a strong writing-is-work ethic that will serve you well if you decide to try to get published. It facilitates progress toward your goals because you're showing up, even on the days you don't feel like it. This is where you capitalize on your writing schedule: when you know that you have to report to your desk from six to eight every evening to write because that's when you scheduled yourself to do so, thinking of it as reporting to a job will help get you there. If it really were your job, you wouldn't blow it off all the time because you'd get fired for that eventually. Just like any other job, you need to show up to write even when you don't feel like it. Stick to your schedule, and then reward yourself for doing so.

For author Jenna Black, cultivating this mindset that writing is a job helped her dig in for the long haul, and she says it was a crucial turning point that led to her success. "For a long time, I simply wrote whenever the urge hit me," she says. "The urge hit me fairly often, so over the course of fourteen years, I managed to write seven books. But when I took a good look at my efforts and reevaluated where I was—which, at the time, was unpublished—I realized I could work a lot harder than I was, and that my chances of seeing my dream come true would be a lot higher if I did. I then dedicated myself to writing, treating it like a job rather than a hobby. I carved out a part of my day that was exclusively dedicated to writing, and I aggressively cleared my schedule so that I could get my writing done."

To aggressively clear your own schedule, use some of the time-management strategies we've already talked about, like doubling up on must-do tasks, compressing tasks, delegating tasks to spouses and older children, or locating time that is naturally obligation free.

Successful Writers Treat Writing Like a Job Before They're Successful

Novelist Sandra Brown treated writing like a job right from the get-go. "I have to say that when I began, I didn't start it as a hobby," she says. "I wasn't going to dabble in it. I thought if I'm going to do this, I'm going to treat it like a job. And that's what I did."

Freelancer Randy Southerland kept his regular job for four years after he began publishing articles in magazines and newspapers. He was writing those articles during most of his off time.

When he finally took the leap to full-time writing, his strong work habits and the attitude that writing was a job helped promote his success. "I got up the next morning and started working at my desk at home," he says, "and I've been doing that ever since. I approach it the same way I did when I had a full-time job—get up early in the morning, be at my desk no later than eight, sometimes earlier, and I work all day."

Novelist Renee Bernard treats her writing like a job, even though she still works part-time jobs to make ends meet. "I think of it like I'm going to work," she says. Bernard's schedule is such that she sets a certain number of hours per week that she has to write (in other words, she uses a time-quota goal), and she thinks of her writing time as punching a time clock. If a part-time job takes away from her writing time one week, she makes up the time by working overtime on her writing.

This mindset is a critical one. "I think one of the keys for writers who aspire to be professional writers, whether writing fiction or nonfiction, is to treat their writing as a business," says freelancer Bruce W. Most. "This doesn't mean simply turning out words as you would widgets. Writing should come from the soul, not the pocketbook. What it does mean is treat your writing 'life' as you would any employer-paid job. If you work for an outside employer, and your hours are nine to five, five days a week, you don't show up at ten, quit at three, and take Fridays off. You get fired for that behavior. So why treat your writing life any differently? Don't take an hour out of the morning to watch TV, vacuum the house, or work in the garden. Establish regular hours and stick to them."

Sacrifices Do Pay Off

Just like starting any other business, the sacrifices will be worth it once the rewards start rolling in. For writers, those rewards come in the form of pages of writing stacking up, check marks on goal tracking sheets, and, eventually, publication.

It takes a while to get the momentum going, but in the end it's worth it. "It's just like when you start a restaurant or any business," says novelist Susan Grant. "The best thing is to expect that it's going to take some years of building it up. It's going to take some years of putting time and money into it, more than you're getting out of it. If you have a healthy attitude, that it's starting a business like any other business, you're much better prepared."

Begin treating your writing like a second job. This is where your writing schedule plays a critical role. You've got that appointment scheduled, so stick to it. If you can only write for fifteen minutes on your lunch break at work, that's okay. The key is to hold yourself accountable to that scheduled writing time. That's how you build the writing habit and create self-discipline.

Also, adopt the perspective that becoming a successful writer will take an investment of time, just like any secondary enterprise that you'd start while also working another job. If you were an accountant and wanted to start a career as a plumber, you wouldn't quit your accounting job without getting the necessary education, learning the required skills, practicing the skills until you mastered them, and creating a sound business plan first. It's the same with writing. Approach it like it's a second job that will eventually be your main source of income (if that is your goal) and that your beginning efforts are an apprenticeship.

chapter eight

The Family/Writing Balancing Act

*B*alancing family life with time to write is not an insurmountable challenge. Successful writers like Merline Lovelace have developed effective strategies for overcoming the distractions of children and other family members being present in the environment while they are writing. These strategies, which we'll cover in this chapter, include creative ways for writing around children, claiming physical space inside the home that is private and used just for writing, setting limits, and creative ways to enlist the support of family members to cooperate with the writing schedule.

Writing Around Children

Many of the writers I interviewed for this book have families, and plenty of them began their writing careers with small children underfoot. Finding time to write with children in the house is a challenge that many writers have successfully faced.

Balancing time to write with a family's needs is a task that has to be interwoven into the fabric of your existing day. This is easy to accomplish when you begin to think of writing as one of your must-do activities at the bottom of your task-prioritization triangle. You start to seamlessly blend writing into your life, and writing and its ancillary activities become a natural part of your day. Folding writing into your life doesn't necessarily mean actually putting words on paper either. Just as you might think about what you need to pick up at the grocery store as you're getting ready to leave your job, successful writers also learn to use the time away from their desks to think about their writing and sort through problems in their heads.

For example, freelance writer Letitia Sweitzer began writing while she was a stay-at-home mom. While she juggled her role of parenting with writing, she developed tricks for capitalizing on the times that she wasn't physically at her desk. "When you have a bunch of children, you're constantly coming and going, picking up children from soccer and such," she says. "I thought a lot about what I was writing when I was driving. I was always thinking that any encounter could lead to an article, any lead was worth thinking about, any place I went was a potential idea. Almost any experience I had, I could turn into an article."

Even when she wasn't at her desk, Sweitzer was thinking about her writing so that when she returned to her work the creative pump was primed. This is a good example of how to make writing part of your lifestyle. Even if you can only write for thirty minutes in the morning, writing can still be a part of the rest of your day. This is one reason why many writers are judicious scribblers—they are prepared at a second's notice to whip out a little notebook and jot down ideas, interesting names, and snippets of dialogue.

Some writers who also care for small children learn to write despite the noise and chaos that children naturally create. Freelancer Vicki Cobb started her career when she was pregnant with her first child, and she simply made accommodations to keep writing after he and a second child were born. "Sometimes I had six little boys in my apartment, running around, screaming and yelling, and that's how I worked," she says. "I can remember a time with my son standing right next to me, screaming for my attention, and I didn't hear him. I'd tuned him out."

Novelist Sherrilyn Kenyon can also go into hyperfocus in a noisy, child-filled environment. "Here's where I was lucky to come from an extremely large and loud family," she says. "I can zone out just about anything. I can even write while watching my sons play hockey. So long as I have a keyboard and can stare into space, I can work."

Like Kenyon, novelist Carly Phillips can also work with lots of activity going on around her. In fact, she uses it to her advantage. "I write with MacBook Pro in my lap, television blaring, and daughters flitting about the house," she says. "Rather than a distraction, I've always worked better with things going on!"

If Children Are a Distraction

Many professional writers have learned to tune out children who are playing nearby while they write. But what if you're the kind of writer who needs more quiet? There are strategies for that too.

Split Child Care with Your Spouse

If you're the type who prefers not to have to keep one eye peeled for the kids while you're also trying to write, approach your spouse about watching the children while you work. Freelance writer Victor D. Chase balanced child-care supervision with his wife's shifts as a nurse so he'd have time to write in the beginning of his career. "My wife went to work at a hospital at the three-to-eleven shift, and I would get up in the morning and do my writing and she'd take care of the kids. Then she'd take off and I'd take over with the kids. Then I would go back to my desk after the kids were in bed and do some more work until she got home at midnight," he says.

It's important to note Chase's last sentence there—not only did he write while his wife watched the kids, he also wrote after the children were asleep on his shift. That's another good example of how to blend writing into your existing day alongside your other obligations.

Hire a Babysitter

If your spouse is unavailable or unwilling to watch the kids while you write, hire out help. Nikoo and Jim McGoldrick (who write as Jan Coffey) began their writing careers at home with two young sons. They hired a babysitter to watch their children while they wrote. "Just because you're home writing doesn't mean you don't need a babysitter," says Nikoo.

Employing a sitter is a useful strategy for balancing your need to write while also caring for children. Alisa Bowman, a freelance writer, tried to work at home for the first year of her daughter's life but found that the routine distractions caused by an infant were not a good match for her writing process, which was more of a Blitz style. "Writing is a very focused activity," she says. "I need big chunks of uninterrupted time. When I realized I couldn't keep working in fifteen-minute bursts, I hired a babysitter two days a week until I could get my daughter into quality daycare."

Write while Kids Are Napping

If your child naps every afternoon from two to three, that may have to be your writing schedule for a while. That's how novelist Renee Bernard did it when her daughter was born. "Anytime she's asleep, I'm trying desperately to feel creative," she says.

When your child is asleep, even though there's probably a million other things that need doing, take the phone off the hook, resist the urge to get sucked into e-mail (for more on this, see Chapter 14), and *write*.

Use Inside Doors with Glass

One secret to learning to write around children (and other family members for that matter) is to train them that when you're writing you're not to be disturbed. As novelist Jim McGoldrick told his kids when he and wife Nikoo were writing, "do not disturb us unless there's blood, bone or smoke." That's one way to say that you have to set limits with your kids, depending on their age, and train them not to disturb you while you're writing. If you have children who need supervision, training them not to interrupt doesn't mean they can't be in the same room or nearby. McGoldrick states that he and Nikoo had French doors with glass installed inside their home so they could shut themselves away from playing children but still be able to see them. A shut door meant Mom and Dad are writing but are nearby in case of emergency.

Use Visual Prompts

With very young children, a good strategy to use is visual prompts. The closed French door is a visual prompt. So are headphones. Novelist Arianna Hart says, "My youngest daughter isn't in school yet, so she knows that if Mommy has the headphones on, she's working."

Another visual prompt you can try with children (this works well with grownups too) is to use red, yellow, and green construction paper to control the "traffic" that wants to intrude on your writing time. This is a trick I learned from a psychologist I used to work with at the community mental health center. She cut circles out of the paper and would tape one of them to her office door according to her availability status. The colors mean the obvious: red indicates do not disturb unless there's a genuine emergency, yellow means come in only if you must, and green stands for it's okay to knock and enter.

Even if you can't shut the door to wherever you're writing because your children are too small, you can still tape the circles on your desk or near your writing table as a visual cue. The different colors will be useful at different stages of your writing and depending on the level of focus you need. For me, green would work if I'm doing research because that's an area I can slip into and out of easily, but red would have to be up when I'm in the actual creative process because I need more concentration at that stage.

Whatever strategy you choose, remember that writing with children around is not an obstacle that has to stop your writing dreams in their tracks.

Put Your Family on Your Writing Schedule

You've put yourself on a writing schedule, and now it's time for your family to fall in line. This is where you may need a healthy dose of attitude, especially if you're family isn't all that supportive of your efforts to write. Or they may be supportive, but because it takes a while to get established as a writer, they may not understand why you continue to persevere. It doesn't matter. The important thing is that *you* believe in you, *you* keep in mind your Vision of Success, *you* work your Writing Action Plan. You decide that you're going to be a writer and hold yourself accountable to that dream. "I have laid the groundwork with friends and family that I was put on this earth to write, so they better make way and let me," says novelist Julia London.

One way you lay the groundwork that London talks about is to keep your writing schedule. If others in your environment consistently see you trotting off to write at the designated time, and you use some of the previously mentioned strategies to minimize interruptions, eventually they'll learn that you really are serious about this. They'll adapt to your new writing schedule just like you do.

Schedules Work Well with Families

The nice thing about a couple of those schedules presented earlier, such as the Early-Morning and After-Hours schedules, is that if you're family isn't supportive at all or won't leave you alone while you're writing, or your spouse won't relieve you of some of the household burdens, fine. You'll write when they're asleep.

Writing while the family is still asleep may be the simplest way to get in your writing time anyway. Somehow it seems easier to go off and write when everyone else is doing something else—in this case, sleeping. It may pan out that you start working that way before you have a family, and you adapt so well that you keep using it after your spouse or children come along.

That's what happened to freelancer Tim O'Shei. He started his Early-Morning schedule before he had a family, and that established routine served him well after he got married and the kids came along. "I still get up around four," he says. "The added challenge is now I'm married. I have two stepchildren and a baby daughter, so that occupies my time as they come first. I find it much more of a challenge now, and I'm more devoted than ever to waking up early and starting the writing at that time."

Set Priorities

The key to balance in any situation is to set priorities. Clearly, the needs of your family, especially small children, have to come first. That's a given. So setting priorities is a key element of success that allows professional writers to balance writing time with family time.

Novelist Susan Grant must make time to write around her job as an airline pilot in addition to her roles as wife and mother. She says that setting priorities helps her juggle the sometimes conflicting demands of being a writer and a parent. "I put my children first, writing second, flying third," she says. "That usually helps in decision making. The [children] come first, so I'm going to have to squeeze writing in at another time. Just like today, I'm on a really bad deadline, but I was invited to speak at my son's school. That doesn't always help me avoid tension, but it helps me avoid guilt."

Remember that writing for a few minutes is better than not writing at all. You may be an Any-Opportunity or a Mini-blocks-of-time writer right now, especially if you have young children at home. So it's critical that you be prepared to write whenever the kids are engaged in something else.

That's how novelist Jodi Picoult did it when her children were small. "When I first started writing, I had a newborn at home, then quickly two more babies. I learned to write any ten minutes I could—when they napped, when they were at preschool, when *Barney* was on TV. I'd park my butt in a chair and write. There were days I wrote garbage, but you can edit garbage. You can't edit a blank page," she says. Doing it this way, you can advance toward your goal of becoming a successful writer and make your kids and family a priority too.

> **"I believe in laying it out to my family that these are my working hours, and that unless there is something extraordinary, do not interrupt me."**
>
> Christine Feehan, *New York Times* bestselling author

Novelist Wendy Corsi Staub says that making her children and their activities a priority also helps her to balance motherhood with a demanding writing career. She has sacrificed many of her leisure activities, at least temporarily, while her children are young. That way she can write and also be there for her kids. "I have two young children, so juggling motherhood with my writing career has made it necessary to give up just about every leisure activity and hobby I used to enjoy, at least during these years while my children need their mom around," she says. "Both my boys play sports, and I make their games and school activities my first priority."

Again, sacrifices like this don't have to be permanent. Children grow up, and over time writers can reinvolve themselves in activities that once fell by the wayside for writing and family time. It may be that all you have time for is your children and your writing. But as your kids get older they need you less, and you can incorporate more of your previous hobbies while also keeping your writing schedule. It's all a matter of balance, time management, and establishing what's important now.

Learning to balance writing time with family life requires skillful time management, and sometimes unforeseen obstacles arise. You may have set aside time to write before the kids arrive home from school, and one day the school nurse calls and you have to spend the afternoon tending to a sick child instead. Or you planned to write every Saturday morning while your significant other gets in his weekly game of tennis, and then he sprains his ankle and can't play for a month. In situations like that, you can either choose another writing schedule on a temporary basis, be flexible and plan to make up the time or the pages at tomorrow's writing session (remember, that's what quota goals are for), or you can simply forge ahead with your writing plans and then get up when you're needed to retrieve juice, fluff a pillow, open a jar, and so forth.

The secret to balance is to attend to what you need to do with your family and blend writing around it. When you approach the situation this way, dealing with those unforeseen obstacles creates less disruption to your overall plan. Writing as a lifestyle means that you can move from one task to the other and back again with ease.

It also helps to remember that becoming a writer is something you are choosing to do. Keeping in mind that being a writer *and* a mom was an intentional choice is how contemporary romance writer Kaitlyn Rice, author of *The Third Daughter's Wish*, balances her multiple roles. "If someone is sick or needs homework help or a ride to the dance, I remember that I made a conscious choice to be a wife and mom. If I want to write with joy, I have to prioritize my time well," she says.

More on Getting Your Family's Support

Achieving a balance between family time and writing time means enlisting your family's support as much as possible. You don't have to have your family's enthusiastic support of your writing endeavors, although it sure helps. The last thing you want to deal with as you're leaving the family room to write is snide comments, complaints, and whining. But you can at least get your family to cooperate as much as possible with your writing schedule.

Post Your Writing Schedule

After you've created your writing schedule, post it in a prominent location in your home and declare your intention to the family that you'll be writing during that designated time. Just come right out and say it. Explain to others in your home that writing equals working. Instruct them that you're not to be disturbed unless there's a true emergency. This is one way that novelist Merline Lovelace solicited her family's help.

"I have my schedule posted on the bulletin board above my computer and when I first started, as things came up, I could point to it and say, 'Sorry, I can't do it, I've got a book due,'" she says.

Leverage the concept of deadlines, because that's something that most people can relate to. Give yourself a deadline to get your writing done, even if you just make one up. In reality you do have a deadline—your long- and your short-term goals. Using those as deadlines to impress upon the family that you really do need to write now is another reason I encouraged you to give them an actual target date for completion. "Post your deadlines," Lovelace says. "It doesn't have to be a deadline for an editor, it could be a deadline for a contest or a self-imposed deadline. Put it up there and let your family see that you've got a deadline you have to meet."

The simple act of stating that you'll be writing at an appointed hour has an immediate effect on others' perceptions of your availability during that time. This is the beauty of setting boundaries—most people respond to them, even if they grouse about it. Lovelace says that her family eventually came to accept—and understand—her writing schedule. "My writing time is my writing time. I guard it very jealously. My family knows it too. Over the years, they've gotten used to it, so that my mornings are mine."

This is another reason why following through with your writing schedule consistently is so important, because it helps others to fall in line. This is how novelist Robyn Carr says that she got her family used to her writing time. "The simplest way to do this is through the use of consistent schedules—no mysteries, no surprises. Once everyone knows you've set aside the hours of one to five P.M. for work, the phone calls stop, no one drops in, everyone just relents," she says.

Make Appointments with Your Family Members

The beauty of a schedule is that just as you pencil in your writing time, you can also make appointments with your family members to spend time with them. If your spouse knows that in one hour you'll be available to go out for that romantic dinner, or you'll be downstairs in thirty minutes to watch the latest *Harry Potter* movie with the family, they're more likely to leave you alone during your one hour of scheduled writing time.

Freelancer and author Cecil Murphey juggled the roles of writer and dad by making a point of spending time with his children each day. "I tried to give my kids my evenings and also some quality time," he says. "Once a month I took the kids, each of them, out for a date. They're in their thirties now, and they still talk a lot about that. It meant a lot to them."

Set Boundaries

You have to set boundaries and take your writing seriously in order to convey that message to others. Remember, you need some attitude. "In addition to setting a schedule, everyone can count on a dash of stubbornness," says novelist Robyn Carr. "If you worked in a bank, no one would expect you to leave work to go shopping or chaperone a field trip."

The attitude of writing equals work can help family members understand why interruptions need to be kept to a minimum. And when your perseverance pays off and you start bringing in money, they *really* understand. "I write at least five days a week, generally six to seven," says novelist Robin Schone. "It helps that my husband works six days a week also. When he's not here it does make it easier, but truthfully, if I have to put a book out and he's here, then that's tough. The fact is that it is a business. My husband knows it's a business. Even though he always respected the writing process, when I started bringing money in he realized, wow, this is more than a vanity thing. And so you have to realize—no write, no money."

Involve Your Family in the Process

Sometimes it isn't easy for people who are not writers to understand your need to lock yourself away on a routine basis to put words on paper, especially in the beginning when success as a writer is still a dream and you're not bringing in cash or getting published.

One way to garner some support from your family is to enlist their help in your writing process. Even though they can't do the actual writing, consider asking them to help in some other way with research, editing, checking for spelling or grammatical errors in your drafts, or reading your stories and giving you feedback. Maybe your spouse knows someone at his or her office who'd be a great source for an article you want to write. Your spouse may be a fountainhead of ideas. Solicit those. If your family feels a part of your process, they can more readily accept your need to write.

Novelist Merline Lovelace has some more great advice on this topic. She says that she involved her family in her writing process by routinely talking about her work and involving her husband with research endeavors. "Right from the start, I involved my family in the process. I'd talk about where I am in a book so they'd know what chapter I was on," she says. "My husband goes with me to conferences and research trips. It's really important to involve your family in the process, and they support you a lot more and they have a stake in it. That's whether you're sold or not sold."

Take Writing Seriously

Enlisting the help of your family may require that you take a look at your attitude toward your writing. Are *you* taking it seriously? When novelist Kimberla Lawson Roby made her dream of writing a priority, that decision inspired her husband and other family members to help. "Writing my first novel became the top priority in my household," she says. "My husband worked a lot of hours but still made sure we had dinner every evening, and my mom came over from time to time to help out with housework, et cetera. They took care of everything, so that I was able to write every evening and every weekend for seven months until my manuscript was complete. This was all while I was still working full time for city government."

How do you start taking your writing seriously? By posting and adhering to your schedule, setting and working toward your goals, and honoring the commitment you've made to your Burning Desire to Write. Don't let yourself down. Declare your intention to become a successful writer. Then others will have no choice but to step aside and let you pass. This is an experience that novelist Rhonda Pollero had. "As soon as I started treating it like very serious, guarded time, everyone else took it that way," she says. "I think a lot of it is how you project it."

Make certain that the attitude you project is that writing time is important to you and that you intend to follow through with your writing schedule and goals. In other words, let your attitude and actions reflect that you're a successful writer and that you write no matter what.

Commandeer Your Own Writing Space

The next key strategy to balancing family with writing is to claim a space in your home that is yours and yours alone. This space should serve only one purpose: writing.

"It's crucial to have a 'place' to work that's yours, and yours alone," says freelance writer Bruce W. Most. "It's not a place for children, spouses, or friends. It's your place, sacrosanct, off-limits to intruders."

Carving out a space at home where you work is as critical as carving out time during the day to write. Novelist L.A. Banks says that laying claim to a small area of her home was how she survived writing while also raising four children. She intentionally chose the laundry room as her writing space for a very practical reason. "I needed space where the kids knew: No you cannot leave your toys here, no you cannot play on mom's computer, no you cannot just barrel in here at will. This is where I work," she says. "I was really adamant about that because I felt like hey, if I've got this little teeny corner by the laundry room, then go, 'That's mine.' And I meant it. And they were cool about it. Who wanted to be in the laundry room? I took the most unattractive space in the house."

Creating a separate writing area also helps you, the writer, transition into writing mode when you step into it. That transition from daily life to writing life will help you make the most of your writing time. Lori Bryant-Woolridge, author of *Hitts & Mrs.* and *Weapons of Mass Seduction*, says that a separate writing space helps her shift mental gears in preparation to write. "Just like athletes will do certain things to mentally prepare their minds to work, so creating a physical environment that when I'm in that space, I'm writing," has been central to her success, she says.

Be on the lookout for space in your home that is not in high demand by other family members. Similar to Banks using the laundry room, John Lescroart, bestselling author of *The Hunt*

Club and *The Suspect*, claimed space for his writing in an area of the house that wasn't attractive to other family members. "I was writing in the mornings, out in the garage, because I had kids," he says. "I literally built a room out there and typed with gloves with holes cut in the fingertips. It was cold. I did that for six years."

Claiming space in the home that will be yours alone and used only for writing is a key element for success. The factor that promotes success is that writing is compartmentalized, so that when you walk into that space you're alerting your creative mind, your family, and yourself that it's time to write. Such a ritual helps get the creative juices flowing and helps you feel more in control of your time and your work.

Balancing home life with time to write is a challenge that successful writers have mastered. It's an ongoing juggling act of prioritizing, scheduling, and managing your time and love for your family with your Burning Desire to Write. Successful writers do it by making time to write part of their lifestyle, and you can too.

chapter nine

The Bottomless Well of Inspiration

a *common question successful writers hear is, "Where do you get your ideas?"* Finding inspiration to make time to write is not a problem for the authors I interviewed. Many of them have more ideas than they can possibly use in a lifetime. All of these ideas inspire them to do one very important thing: make even more time to write.

In this chapter, we'll cover where bestselling authors like Carla Neggers and Sandra Brown find and develop their ideas. Many writers mine their own lives, jobs, and experiences for topics. They turn ordinary events into writing material. They capitalize on their unique perspective of the world, just like you can do.

Everyone has a unique slant on life. Ten people can witness the same event, yet they'll tell ten different stories. This is good news for aspiring writers. It means that even if a story idea has been done before, there's something fresh that you can bring to it.

Having many ideas inspires writers to make time to write, and it creates motivation to get those ideas down on paper. You know the feeling: an idea for a book or article seizes you, and because of your enthusiasm for the topic, you're inspired to write about it.

Ideas Start Small and Grow

There's no shortage of ideas, even if a similar theme has already been written about. Successful writers in all genres are always on the lookout for new story ideas, or fresh angles to stories already told, and their imaginations are always on overdrive.

"I have a vivid imagination," says novelist Carla Neggers. "I remember crossing this little chain link bridge in Chattanooga up on Lookout Mountain. I was crossing it with my father-in-law, and we're looking down. I looked at him and said, 'Gee I wonder what would happen if this bridge came apart?' He said, 'Why do you have to think that way?' And I said, 'I just do.'"

Professional writers often take that "what would happen if" scenario that Neggers talks about to the extreme. "'What would happen if?' That's how I start out," she explains. "For the book *The Rapids*, I was visiting cousins in Holland and we were doing the tour of a canal-like waterway that goes underneath buildings. The whole tour was in Dutch, and I have very limited abilities in Dutch, so I'm going along thinking, 'I wonder what would happen if a dead body floated by? And what if it was an American?' And next thing you know, I have a book. I do come with this vivid imagination, so that's my main inspiration, and I love to write."

Many successful writers discover that ideas for books and articles begin with a single thought that grows as they think about and consider it. You've probably had this experience yourself. "A little hook of an idea will start tugging at my imagination," says novelist Mary Jo Putney. "You get little ideas and your brain kind of chews on them like a dog with a bone. You need to find a way to make sense of it."

When you find yourself asking, "What if?" or turning a gem of an idea over and over in your head, you're on to an article or story idea. Write it down and flesh it out. If you're curious as to why a particular event happened a certain way, why a solution to a problem has never been found, or what would happen if a dead body floated by in a river, then you are the writer to ferret out that information and present it to the world. If you're curious about something, chances are lots of other people are too. Use your natural interest to motivate you to make time to write about it, and be the one to put pen to paper. Get an article or book out of it. Even research can be fun when you are learning about a topic that interests you, and watching a fictional story unfold beneath your hands can bring you, the writer, as much joy and entertainment as it will to the eventual reader. Use your natural curiosity and your Burning Desire to Write to its full advantage. Let your imagination run wild.

Ideas Come from Everywhere

Look around at what's going on in the world, in your neighborhood, and in your own backyard. "I find inspiration everywhere," says novelist Roxanne St. Claire. "I read several newspapers a day, I watch documentaries, I ask people their life stories and listen to the answers. Inspiration is not hard to find if you are open to it."

The trick is to keep your ears perked up and listen out for ideas during your daily routine. "I get my ideas from the most mundane places," says freelance writer Sally Abrahms. She even gets ideas while getting her hair cut. "I was sitting next to a woman who had a great story about her uncle who was a ninety-five-year-old artist. When you're talking to somebody, ideas come," she says.

"Anything can spark an idea for a book," agrees Rebecca Brandewyne, the bestselling author of *The Crystal Rose*. "A piece of music, a news story, a snatch of conversation, whatever. Most writers are chock-full of story ideas, so it's really a matter of sifting through them all and determining which ones will make the best books."

As you practice listening out for ideas during your daily routine, you'll start to develop an intuition about where to look for ideas. Freelance writer Jennifer Haupt has developed a knack over the years for finding great human interest stories. She says she just learned to know where to look. "You develop sources in all different places, and if you're interested in a certain kind of story, then you're going to do research on that and start getting contacts in places, or I'll hear something on the radio," she says.

As you begin to develop leads on story ideas, your knowledge base expands and you start making connections in the world that can help you find or research future stories. Freelance writer David Axe says he keeps his ears perked up for ideas during ordinary conversations, and he'll also follow up with sources he's talked to in the past when scouting for new article ideas. "I read a lot, keep in touch with expert sources, and try to mine every article and conversation for ideas that might turn into stories," he says. You can do this too as you start to step out and gain experience in the world of writing.

Successful writers learn through practice what ideas will resonate with editors. As they continue to pitch stories, it refines their ability to spot trends and hot topics. "When I first started out," says freelancer Karen Asp, "it was catch-as-catch-can. I sent off-target pitches.'"

Over time, says Asp, as her knowledge and understanding of her specialty deepened, she could spot trends more easily, and maintaining her fitness certifications helps her generate fresh article ideas. "The thing that made writing possible was that I found this specialty and I became very knowledgeable in this topic. Therefore, I could craft the pitches a little bit better," she says. "I'm constantly going and hearing about the latest and greatest workouts and things like that. I can generate tons of ideas because I still have to attend workshops and conferences to keep my certification."

Inspiration can spring out of any situation—anytime, anywhere. Most professional fiction writers are always on the lookout for story ideas. "I tend to get inspiration from just about anywhere," says novelist Gemma Halliday. "I love to watch television, and I tend do a lot of what-ifing, rewriting the endings of shows, dreaming up back story for some of the characters, or picking out a minor character and imagining what his story must be."

With So Many Ideas, How Do Professional Writers Choose?

Because successful writers usually have more ideas than they can ever write about in a lifetime, how do they decide which ones they'll actually use? Debbie Macomber, the bestselling author of *Back on Blossom Street* and *74 Seaside Avenue,* has a unique approach. "I came up with a guideline of four words," she says, "and every idea is aligned with these four words." Macomber's four words for choosing which ideas to develop into novels are:

- The story must be *relevant* to her readers.
- She must be able to tell the story in an *honest* way.
- She must be able to tell the story in a *creative* way that brings different plots together.
- The story must be *compelling*.

Kids Aren't Disruptions, They're Idea Machines

The wonderful part about being a writer-parent is that kids are bottomless wells of article and story ideas. The time you spend parenting can be converted into gold when you sit down to write, since your creative pump should be primed.

"I would say to [aspiring writers] who have kids, exploit them ruthlessly in all media," jokes Greg Daugherty, a freelance writer and editor. Daugherty has written about some of his parenting experiences and qualifies his comment by adding that he would often let his children review what he'd written about them "if there was any possibility that they'd be mortified."

Children can create opportunities for ideas that would have never presented themselves before. "I started out in public relations," says freelancer Jennifer Haupt. "When my first son was born, I decided I wanted to freelance. I started writing for local parenting magazines and a baby diaper service magazine." After earning a few credits, Haupt turned her attention to *Parents* magazine and wrote for that publication as well.

Children provide writers lots of anecdotal stories. An anecdote is a short, interesting story about a real person or event, and you've probably noticed that many articles in magazines begin this way. Professional writers often use their own personal life experiences for these stories, and kids are a great source.

Freelancer Sandra J. Gordon blends her experiences as a mom into her work using her kids for anecdotes. "For example, I wrote a piece for *Parents* which discussed the science of genetics," she says. "In the lead, I started out with the birth of my first daughter. She was a brunette, although I'm blond and my husband's a redhead. How'd that happen? That sort of thing. For a piece on C-sections, also for *Parents*, in the lead I mentioned my own C-section. For my *Consumer Reports* book, *Best Baby Products*, I wove my own experience with baby products into the text throughout the book."

Being a parent and a writer are not mutually exclusive experiences. You can use the novel experiences that kids give you to create stories and article ideas too. Capitalize on your parenting experiences, and use them to advance toward your dream of becoming a writer.

> **"I've often described my brain as one of those domed toddler push toys, with all the bright colorful balls bouncing around. I see those balls as ideas. Whenever I'm between books, I pluck out a ball, and that becomes my story."**
>
> JoAnn Ross, *New York Times* bestselling author

On-the-Job Experience Equals Ideas

Since you spend so much of your life at a job, why not capitalize on that by using your experiences there to generate ideas for books and articles. You have certain skills, talents, and perspectives that people who are not in the field don't have. That unique perspective will appeal to editors. "Most people are coming from something—they've been out there working—so I say leverage what you know," says Peter Bowerman, a commercial copywriter and author of The *Well-Fed Writer* series.

Your job experiences also make you an expert on that subject, something else that will appeal to editors. I once tried for about a year to break in with a regional magazine. I sent many queries over that period of time. I didn't have any success until the editor herself came across an idea for an article: it was a human interest piece about a little boy with autism who had created a line of greeting cards. She asked me to write the article because I'm a licensed counselor, a fact that I had repeatedly mentioned in my queries. Technically, any writer could have done that article, but because of my expertise, it was a match in the editor's mind, and she gave me the assignment.

Using on-the-job experience is valuable for fiction writers too. Novelist Rick Mofina, who worked as a crime reporter, used his experiences of talking to cops and seeing life and death up close in his writing. He selected elements of his job that appealed to him emotionally to write about. "I stepped back and thought about what motivates me in terms of story, and what were the ones that got to me." he says.

Whether it be job, kids, or reporting on a unique human interest story in their community, many writers got their start when they discovered that the best, and richest, ideas are often found close to home. "People should look for something that they can deliver that nobody else can," advises freelance writer and editor Greg Daugherty. "If there's something going on in your part of the country that an editor in New York may not know about, that's great. If you're a woodworking hobbyist and you can explain that clearly to people in an article, use that information to generate queries," he suggests. "Look to where you live and what you know that others may not know."

Freelance writer Victor D. Chase used job experience to kick off a career in science writing. He worked at an institute that was involved in energy research. "I became familiar with all sorts of energy technology: solar, wind, hydrogen fuel cells, et cetera," he says. Chase then transferred this knowledge to writing. "Since I had an expertise in alternative energy technology, I started writing about all sorts of energy conservation in building," he says. "I've always been interested in science and how things work, writing is my real love, and I combine the two."

It's not difficult to do. Just take a look at your current and past jobs, even ones you had as a teenager, and make a list of all the topics you could write about based on your knowledge. For example, freelance writer Kevin Garrison turned his unique job skills, knowledge, and know-how as a pilot into more than eight hundred published articles. "I used my status as an airline pilot to get into a lot of magazines because I was a so-called expert," he says. "I've been an instructor for twenty-five years, so I've sold a lot of articles based on the fact that I was an instructor, combined with the fact that I was an airline pilot, because my audience has always been interested in what it's like to fly a 727."

Tara Dillard, a professional garden designer who has written five books, including *The Garden View: Designs For Beautiful Landscapes*, says that for her, finding time to write comes naturally because she's always inspired and passionate about her topic. "My thinking is, if somebody wants to be a writer, they have to be as crazy into that topic as I am into my gardening. My advice is, just go overboard on what you love and what you're writing about."

Sit down and make a list of everything you know. Brainstorm. Don't hold back. Draw on your life, work, and family experiences. From that list, create a second list with as many topic ideas under each subject as you can generate. You'll be amazed at how much is in your head. The list will probably be much longer than you think, and you can use the subjects as a jumping off place at your next writing session.

Capitalize on Your Unique Perspective

We all have our backgrounds, family histories, and life experiences that color how we interpret events and information. Everybody has a unique perspective on the world, even on similar events. This opens up a wide field of opportunity for aspiring writers, because even if a story has been done before, chances are very good that you can bring something different to the topic.

Novelist Susan Grant says that writing about heroines who were airline pilots, which is her profession, was a key element to her success. "Right away I tied what I wrote to what I do. You know, 'My unique experience is…'," she says. "Now my books have branched off, but the common element is some of the things I've done in my life: the airline, the military, the travel, the fact that I was a pilot. I put that in my book."

Your unique perspective is usually found in what you feel passionate about. What world events or happenings in your neighborhood get you fired up? What makes you angry? What makes you shout for joy? There's your passion; there's your unique perspective on a situation. There's where you need to place your focus during your writing times.

Professional writers are often inspired to make time to write about topics they feel strongly about. "With nonfiction, you're really passionate about ideas and seeing those ideas come together, whereas for fiction, you're passionate about the work itself because it's yours," says freelance writer and editor Alix Strauss. "It's gut-wrenching, heart-wrenching, it's your material, it's everything that's you. Whereas with nonfiction, I really love being able to find a story and being able to be clever or hunt something down or see something differently than somebody else would."

Novelist Pamela Morsi says that with her interest in historical as well as contemporary fiction she's learned to listen for unusual ideas in the news and from other people. She then creates a unique slant on the information to formulate her book ideas. "I love taking a problem or issue that we think about today and transposing that issue into another time period," she says.

Successful writers can usually generate multiple ideas from a given category, and again, it's because the topics are fascinating to them personally. This is the approach that motivates Marla Paul, a freelance writer and author of *The Friendship Crisis: Finding, Making, and Keeping Friends When You're Not a Kid Anymore*. "Things that I find funny or outrageous or wrong inspire me," she says. "Also, if I'm struggling with something personally, that often sparks an essay. I may write an essay on my struggles as a mom or an outrageous fashion trend or my terrible gardening. Writing helps me figure things out."

Ideas feed off of each other, including those for fiction and nonfiction. "Several of my ideas for fiction have come from my nonfiction writing," says freelance writer and novelist Bruce W. Most. "For example, I'm currently working on a murder mystery that revolves around contemporary cattle rustling. In part, the idea grew out of the fact I have in-laws who are working ranchers. But it also grew out of a couple of published articles I wrote over twenty years ago on modern-day cattle rustling. That idea just stuck in the back of my head."

Generate a list of what is unique about you. What is your angle on every subject that you already have some knowledge or expertise in? What fresh slant can you bring to an old idea? Put your unique spin on your ideas. Maximize your expertise in any given area by using it to generate article ideas.

Add to this list over time and use it as a working document that inspires you to make time to write. Be alert for those blips of inspiration you get throughout the day—write them down, put your unique spin on them, and make time to write about them. The topics can act as prompts that give you a jump-start on days when you struggle to get words on paper. A good way to overcome writer's block is to have a ready-made list of ideas that you can pull from to get you started. When you arrive at your desk, pull out your list and use it to kick your muse into high gear.

Psychology 101: Universal Themes

Personal life issues are another area where ordinary people who became successful writers have found inspiration to make time to write. Something affects you deeply, and because you're a writer you want to write about it. Have you had to cope with major illness, aging parents, or watched a sibling or child go off to war? What skeletons lurk in your family closet that writing about might help heal yourself and others? One great thing about writing is that no matter what your unique situation, it's very likely that there are other people who have experienced something similar. Reading about how other people have coped with a painful problem can be wonderfully healing and comforting. In psychology this is often referred to as a problem having a universal theme. It means that most people can relate either to the problem itself or to the suffering that is attached to it, even if they haven't experienced precisely the same thing. It's the idea that despite our differences we're all in the same boat of humanity. Whatever you're feeling or dealing with in your own life, there's a good chance that someone out there wants to read about how you have lived with it.

Writing about situations that are normally taboo is a challenge that Kathyrn Harrison, author of three memoirs, including *The Kiss* and *Seeking Rapture*, has embraced. "The fact that I'm honest—to a fault, some might say—is central to my success," she says. Harrison adds that her willingness to be forthcoming about subjects ordinarily shrouded in secrecy, such as incest, and her complex relationships with her parents has made her work valuable to certain readers.

You already have the inspiration in the form of your life experiences, your unique perspective and what you know. Sit down at your desk at your appointed time and write about it.

Writing Begets Writing

The more you write, the more ideas you get, which in turn makes you want to write even more. Once you get an idea, it creates offshoots and tangents that offer up more story lines. Original themes often transform into more specific angles or interesting plots once you see them in writing and play with them.

"When I first begin, I come up with the plot, and this takes a few months usually to get all the details hammered out," says novelist Sandra Brown. "Some books are much, much easier than others in plotting. Sometimes the plot comes fully blown and I know exactly where it's going and what's going to happen, and other times I'll come up with an idea and I'll sit and hammer it and hammer it for weeks until I get to that Ah-ha! That's what it needed, that was the element that made it all come together."

Brown adds that sometimes ideas may not blossom into story ideas immediately. "Some ideas simply do not want to become plots," she says. "They just don't. They dig their heels in and you have to say, 'Good idea but it didn't work,' and get on to something else. I may come back to it later when something new occurs to me."

> "I have more ideas than I could ever get to in my lifetime, and new ones assault me constantly."
>
> Sherrilyn Kenyon, *New York Times* bestselling author

Because the creative well is constantly refilling, time to write is something that professional writers often look forward to each day. "I have never had a problem with actually thinking up story lines," says novelist Christine Feehan. "I have a very vivid imagination, and there's always a book in the back of my head, even when I'm writing the one I'm concentrating on."

Novelist Hallie Ephron points out that new ideas will often form when a writer is finishing up a project, which then creates motivation to find time to write for the next story. "An idea incubates for a while without you being aware that it's incubating, hopefully while you're finishing the previous project," she says.

Research Time Creates Ideas

If your writing time is partially spent doing research, capitalize on that by generating as many ideas out of the research as possible. Make a list of more article or story ideas as you go along to provide yourself with a constant stream of new topics. "Often what happens is previous stories lead to new ideas," says freelance writer Laura Fraser. "You'll find some angle or topic that you've already covered in a different story, or perhaps it works for a different magazine. So things kind of branch out."

Since your writing time may be brief, maximize on time spent at writing-related tasks by getting as many ideas as possible out of that exploratory session. That way, once you sit down to write you already have a starting point and a plan. Having a plan will motivate you to get to your desk and work. You don't have to dread the upcoming writing session; you have a plan, and you can jump right in.

For example, Sandra J. Gordon is always on the lookout for spinoff ideas whenever she's researching a particular topic. "Something else will come out of any kind of research that will help me make another query," she says.

Gordon also looks over the raw material (interviews and research notes) from past pieces when generating new article ideas. She explains that since she always includes at least one quote and one statistic in every query letter, the in-depth work that she's already done on the topic pays off because more ideas can be culled from old information.

"I never start from scratch," Gordon says. "I always start from interviews that I have that can be mined for something else. I might stare at it for a while to get an angle, but rarely do I do fresh interviews for queries."

Review your own original material and recycle it to generate more ideas. When you interview or talk to someone, actively think of additional stories you can glean from that one conversation.

"Sometimes you just take a story and respin it in a way that might be surprising," says freelancer Sally Abrahms. She gives as an example a piece she did on seniors who sang on a rock-and-roll tour. One of the men was a retired medical doctor, so she reslanted the original piece and sold it to the man's alma mater. "I take an original story and figure out what I can use again," she says.

This also works in fiction. Researching an idea is how novelist Robin Schone fleshes out her stories. "When you're researching something, you get a feel for it," she explains. "I'll come across a key element and it will call to me. The character will spring out of that."

When you research a topic, print all the materials, including the URL, and keep everything in a file that you can refer back to later (becoming a pack rat is an occupational hazard for writers). It's often difficult to find that exact article or research study on the Internet at a later time. Printing everything allows you to relocate the article again quickly if you need to, and you'll always have potential writing topics to reach for when you arrive at your desk. Storing hard copies of research materials will save you time in the long run.

How to Find Real People for Anecdotes

If you're writing an article that requires real, live people for anecdotes, ask your local librarian to show you how to find information on current research studies using your library's database.

(Librarians are gold mines of information.) Then enlist the help of physicians or other researchers who are involved in those studies to find people interested in providing the anecdotal material that you need. You can usually locate the researchers by contacting the university or hospital named in the study. "If someone is studying a particular area you're trying to cover, they have all the patient information and all that they have to do is tap into the people in their study," says freelancer Sandra J. Gordon. Gordon used this approach recently when she needed to find a mother and daughter who were trying to quit smoking at the same time, and the daughter had to be a teenager of a very specific age.

All You Need Is One Good Idea

In my writing classes, aspiring authors always ask about the importance of clips in terms of getting noticed by an editor or agent. Clips are copies of previously published material. I've got good news for you—you don't need them to break in, although many people think you do. It's that old dilemma: you can't get a job without experience, and you can't get experience without a job. But the truth is, if you've got a good idea and you present it in a professional looking and sounding query letter, chances are you'll break in.

The primary thing you need is one good idea. Look for something that you can deliver that nobody else can. In other words, use your unique perspective to create one good idea. What can you bring to a topic that nobody else has brought?

"When an editor's looking at an idea of yours," explains writer Greg Daugherty, "they're looking at two things: one is the idea, the other is whether or not you're the right person to do it." What makes you the right person is your unique slant on the world.

Freelancer Sally Abrahms successfully broke into women's magazines not because she was an experienced writer but because she used her unique perspective on life to generate good ideas: "I started writing for the women's magazines because I had the ideas. People think you have to have all these clips, and what I found was that if I had a really good story idea and I could do it, they didn't care what my credentials were."

Ideas for new stories are never in short supply. All of these ideas motivate writers to make time to write. Capitalizing on their unique lives and perspectives in order to generate new material is another way that professional writers constantly fulfill their Burning Desire to Write. They have found ways to access the source of their creativity. You can too.

chapter ten

Tap into the Wellspring of Creativity: Your Subconscious Mind

*M*otivational leaders often speak of the power of the *subconscious mind* as an inexhaustible source of answers and information that we do not have access to on a conscious level. Many successful writers, like bestselling novelist Ann Major, actively use techniques designed to access their subconscious minds as a way of helping stimulate the creative process, to come up with ideas, to solve problems in the story, and to improve their writing. In this chapter, I'll show you ways to build a bridge to your own subconscious mind.

To clarify, your conscious mind is what you use to think with day-to-day. It's the thinking portion of your mind that is readily available for use in an alert state. The conscious mind keeps your daily life running, and running well. It tells you when it's time to pay the bills, it keeps you from stepping out in front of moving cars, it helps you know how to safely operate the stove, it provides logical thinking so that you can answer questions and perform on your job, and so forth. The subconscious is what's just beneath the surface of conscious thought. It's the storehouse of all your memories, feelings, and knowledge. It's like a virtual psychic warehouse of all of your life experiences. There are easy ways to access this wellspring of creativity that can help you when you get stumped or the flow of your writing dries up or stops. The most obvious but most overlooked way is simply to ask.

Freelance writer Vicki Cobb often does this when she's writing poetry. "I tell myself, 'You have to write a poem on such and such a subject,' and I give it a deadline, and then I leave it alone," she says. Cobb explains that over the next few days, she'll get inklings here and there of how the poem should read. She calls this the gestation period that precedes a major breakthrough of ideas, and then there comes a moment where there's so many ideas she has to put them down on paper.

Novelist Ann Major also uses the strategy of asking for help from her subconscious mind. "I give my brain an assignment," she explains. "I say, 'Okay, why is he upset about this? What do I need to have happen here?' I put those questions [to my mind], I write them down, and it's amazing what answers will come to me."

Here are some more tips for accessing that bottomless well of ideas that is yours for the asking:

- Write down a question prior to going to sleep and ask your subconscious mind to provide you with the answer in the morning.
- Keep a writing pad beside your bed to record dreams and middle-of-the-night ideas.

Most dreams occur in REM (rapid eye movement) sleep, but because this is the deepest phase of sleep, people forget most of them. Yet this is the brain's most creative time. In one study, people were awakened abruptly during REM sleep and shown a set of cards; the stories that they told were more vivid than the ones they generated after non-REM sleep. You can train yourself to capture ideas from REM sleep by recording them as soon as you wake up in the morning or during the night. This is a habit that strengthens over time and helps build a connection between your sleeping and waking minds.

> **"Sometimes ideas come to me in the middle of the night."**
>
> Jennifer Haupt,
> freelance writer

- File a question or a problem in your subconscious mind and then forget about it. When the answer is ready, it will come to you.
- Carry a notebook or minirecorder with you at all times. As you become attuned to it, your subconscious will offer suggestions in the form of ideas when you're not at your desk. Be ready to capture them.
- Take a break from your writing. As you'll see in Chapter 12, taking a break can be helpful at times when it's warranted. Sometimes a short break is all it takes for your mind to work out a problem. "If I take a break—going for a walk, working in my yard or doing mindless-type knitting—my subconscious often solves the problem and writing resumes," says novelist Jennifer Blake.

The source of creativity is your subconscious mind. Using these strategies, you can access that bottomless well of ideas just like professional writers.

chapter eleven

Ways to Write Even When You Don't Feel Like It

ven though ideas are endless, there are the occasional days when writers feel uninspired to work or are intimidated by the blank page. Their schedule is in place, and writers arrive at their desk at the designated time to write, but the inspiration to actually write has tapered off. What do professional writers do in these situations?

In this chapter, we'll review strategies from bestselling authors like Catherine Coulter and Connie Brockway on how they square off with the blank page and get their writing done, even on days when they don't feel like it.

Don't Wait for the Muse

Even though professional writers have ways of accessing the source of their creativity, ways that you now have too, they don't wait around for the muse to show up in order to start writing. For them, writing is a habit. They write no matter what. They show up. They sit down at their desks at the scheduled writing time and put their fingers on the keyboard. That's why they can write, even on days when they may not feel particularly creative. While it's nice when divine inspiration strikes and drives you to your desk, the hallmark of a professional writer is that even when they don't feel like it, they write anyway.

This is the strength of the writing schedule: you've got your appointed hour, you go to your desk, you get your writing time in, and then you're done for the day. There's really no other way to accomplish this feat other than to exercise a healthy dose of self-discipline. But here's a secret: the self-discipline muscle strengthens the more you use it, and the more you write, the more writing becomes a habit.

"To be honest here, inspiration or the muse haven't played much of a role in selecting what I'm going to write about," says Catherine Coulter, bestselling author of *Point Blank*, *Double Take*, and other suspense, romance, and thriller novels. "The famous muse is scarce, if it exists at all. What a writer does, if success is desired, is keep firmly planted in the computer chair for the same hours every single day, and writing. Put me in a closet, it simply doesn't matter. A writer writes. I write."

Successful writers write no matter what. This means writing even on days when the muse fails to show. "When it's a writing day, I'm writing. Period," says novelist Jodi Picoult. "It's not about waiting for a muse, it's about dedication and hard work." Her comment hearkens back to the strength of a writing schedule and holding yourself accountable. You've got that writing schedule in place, and the only thing to do is work it. If you consistently fail to follow through, examine why. If you chose the Early-Morning schedule but your brain is simply mush at that time, try the After-Hours schedule. If you can't meet your quota goal, figure out why not. Maybe you're quota goal doesn't match your individual creative process. Change to another one. But by all means, don't give up. Try various schedules and quota goals until you find what clicks for you and your creativity, and then stick with it. Remember, writing is a job, even if it's not a paid job.

"You can't wait for inspiration or the muse to show up if you want to become a successful commercial fiction writer," agrees novelist Vicki Lewis Thompson. "You work at it with the same dedication as you would any job."

Sometimes the Hardest Part is Just Getting Started

A typical problem that many writers experience is beginning a writing session when the engine is cold, so to speak. You're not in the mood to write. Or you sit down, open up the file you're working on, hover your pen over your notebook, and it feels like you're brain just isn't on. You can think of a million other ways you'd like to be spending that hour.

The successful tactic many writers use for dealing with days that they felt this way is to simply exercise self-discipline and start writing just to get the juices flowing. Self-discipline is an art form, and the only way to master it is to practice it. But it pays off, because after the seemingly monumental feat of just getting to the desk is over with, the act of telling the story will usually generate the inspiration to write after a writer has disciplined herself to sit down.

After the powerful act of just beginning, successful writers report that the love of writing, or their Burning Desire to Write, reappears. Charlene Ann Baumbich, a freelance writer and novelist, says that the anticipation and joy of finding out what will happen next in the story is what motivates her to get to her desk. "I'm a story chaser," she says. "I don't know what's going to happen. Curiosity and really interesting people drive me. If I got up and knew what was going to happen, I probably would not enjoy writing fiction."

Getting lost in her make-believe worlds is what keeps novelist Merline Lovelace at her desk on days when she may not feel inspired. "I love being able to create all these huge imaginary worlds and watch the characters come to life," she says. "So it's kind of a self-fulfilling prophecy. It *is* work, and there's days when you think, 'Oh god, I don't want to do this.' But once you get into it and you get lost in those other worlds, it's just so much fun."

The Burning Desire to tell a story from beginning to end is what motivates novelist C.J. Lyons to fill blank pages. "Since I don't plot ahead of time, I'm just as surprised by where the story ends up as my audience. So if I can surprise myself and create a compelling world where the characters come to life, then I have plenty of motivation to stick with it," she says.

Specific Techniques to Make Writing Happen

You've gotten to the desk at your scheduled writing time, and there you are, at the blank page. How do you fill it? First, congratulate yourself for showing up! That's over half the battle. Now you need to start writing. There are a variety of strategies that writers use to jump-start the process: editing, researching, outlining, and writing hard and fast.

Work on Plot Points or Character Development

One way to get started with your writing when you don't feel motivated is to work on background elements, like plot points. Jennifer O'Connell, author of *Off the Record* and *Bachelorette #1*, has a good technique for accomplishing this task: she constructs the major plot points of her book on a monthly, one-page calendar when she's first starting out. She does this, she says, because she knows how her books start, she knows how they end, but she doesn't know what happens in the middle. Using the one-page, one-month calendar also allows her to see the whole book laid out in big-picture form, and she can see the timeline, which she believes is important to keep. "Picture a one-month calendar, and every square is a chapter. I write down the four highlights of the chapter, just the major things," she says. "Keeping an eight-and-a-half-by-eleven page, with a bunch of squares that are chapters, allows me to go in and cut and paste and move things. I can see everything that happens in the book."

Working on your characters is also a good strategy for kicking your writing process off when you feel sluggish. Novelist Sabrina Jeffries likes to flesh out her characters as a way to fill blank pages, and she says it helps her cut down on revisions later since she gets her characters squared away in the beginning of the book. "I have a character checklist I've invented over time because I always have the same things that are up in the air when I start a book, and that's why I end up revising so much," she says. "So I'm trying now to think through those things before, and it's cut down on my revisions, but it hasn't eliminated them." Jeffries graciously gave me permission to share her checklist with you—you can find it in Appendix C.

Write a Synopsis

Some writers like to begin work with a detailed synopsis of their story. This is how Kat Martin, bestselling author of *Heart of Honor* and *The Secret*, fills her blank pages. "I write a long synopsis, twenty-five to thirty pages," she says. "I write dialogue and everything in there. It reads like a short story. The longer the synopsis, the better the book is, I think."

A synopsis may or may not reveal all the plot points of the book. It depends on the writer's individual creative process. For instance, novelist Sandra Brown writes a synopsis, then starts writing even if she doesn't know exactly how everything in the story will pan out. "I know where my characters need to go and I give them a little bit of direction, but a lot of it I want to just come out of the writing. So I just let them take over the story at that point. In other words, I know where they're going, I don't always know how they're going to get there," she says.

Brown explains that she knows the essential events of the book, and after she completes her synopsis she will highlight those to make sure they're included when she writes. But there are still times in the writing when she is surprised or something happens in the book that she didn't see coming. Notice how she uses the "What if?" question. "Sometimes I'll get to a point and say, 'Wait a minute, what if this happens?'" she says. "But I don't do a scene-by-scene or chapter-by-chapter outline, or I would have written the book. There wouldn't be any challenge for me then."

Outlining and Breaking Projects into Small Pieces

Outlining and breaking projects into small, manageable pieces is a useful time-management strategy, but it's amazing how often we forget to do this as way of getting started if we feel paralyzed by the amount of work we face. Especially for aspiring writers who have to work other jobs, or have major responsibilities that force them to write in small chunks of time, outlining can be an especially useful strategy for capitalizing on your writing time.

Breaking a large project into smaller pieces is a technique that freelancer Alisa Bowman uses. "For example," she says, "I'm editing a book right now that is due next week. I figured that I need to edit about four thousand words a day to hit the deadline. When I'm writing a book, I set chapter deadlines for myself."

Working backwards like that and figuring out how much work you should produce during your scheduled writing time to meet your long-term goal's deadline should be your short-term-quota goal. If you want to write a four-hundred-page novel in twelve months, you need to write approximately thirty-three pages per month, or eight pages per week to meet that goal. If you write three times a week, that's two to three pages per session.

More traditional outlining is another good way to fill blank pages and generate enthusiasm for a project. An outline can also give you a short-term-quota goal to work on. Simply use the sections of your outline as your goal for that day.

For instance, if chapter one has three plot points, on Monday, Tuesday, and Wednesday your quota goal will be to write a draft of those three plot points during your scheduled writing time. If chapter two has four plot points, on Thursday and Friday the quota goal will be to flesh two out.

Outlining a project from beginning to end gives you a road map to follow and helps point you in the right direction. When you sit down to write, you've got a plan in place that will make getting started easier. You won't dread going to your desk because you know what you need to do and you can just start.

"I find that if I'm flailing around," says writer and editor Greg Daugherty, "if I can find the structure of what I want to say, it helps a great deal. I'll type on the computer screen the high points I want to hit, and the order I want to hit them, and then start to fill in each section from there."

Daugherty says that this approach works especially well if the idea he's trying to get on paper is cloudy and amorphous. "You go in and do the pieces of it you can first, then try to put it all together," he says. "Then go back through it at the end and make sure it all hangs together all right."

Novelist Hallie Ephron has a unique use for her outlines. She revises the outlines instead of her work in progress and uses them as a true road map for plotting and guiding her writing process. "When I do a major revision, the way I do it is by looking at the outline," she says. "So I'll be reading the book, but annotating the outline. Somehow, having the revisions on the outline instead of the book makes it easier to revise. I read the book but I edit the outline, and then I revise."

Outlines provide encouragement for you to get to your desk because they create a safety net—you don't have to arrive clueless at the blank page, you have your outline there to guide you. Even if you revise later, at least you didn't sit in front of your monitor, agonizing because you had nothing to say. Professional writers will take revisions over a blank page any day of the week.

A TV Trick: Write a Treatment

Novelist Lori Bryant-Woolridge utilizes her extensive experience that she gained in television work when she begins a new book. She starts out by writing what she calls a treatment. She explains that a treatment "is the running story without the dialogue—what happens in the beginning, middle, and end." Similar to a synopsis, a treatment tells the whole story in one swoop. The difference is that unlike a synopsis, a treatment is then broken down into plot points and chapters. And, unlike a synopsis where surprises may occur in the writing, Bryant-Woolridge explains that "you have to leave the flexibility for new information, but you always feel like you're in control."

Stop in the Middle

One of the key elements required for setting yourself up for writing success is to have a plan for when you sit down at your desk. You don't want to sit there squirming around, humming and staring at the ceiling, during your writing time (unless thinking is part of your plan—sometimes writers do need to sit there and think about plot development). Knowing where to start the next writing session is a good way to make sure that you can jump right in and get going and make the most use of your precious time.

"I always try to stop work for the day in the middle of a chapter that's going really well, so that I can look forward to going back to work the next day," says novelist Hilary Norman. This is an innovative technique that works for many writers.

Connie Brockway, bestselling author of *Hot Dish* and other novels, has another trick. She uses an After-Hours schedule and will intentionally leave off in the middle of a scene so that she has a place to pick up the next evening. She explains that she tries to finish one scene and then begin a new one, then she stops. "If

I go to bed with a scene just beginning, it unfolds in my imagination over the night," she says. "It steeps like a tea bag in my imagination while I'm sleeping, and I have something to grab onto the next morning. I push the stone off the top of the hill, so to speak, and it's begun to roll down. It's very hard for me to get up and start a cold scene without having a little momentum to start me."

Write Anything

One time honored trick that professional writers use to tackle the blank page is to simply start writing—anything. Sometimes when you freeze up at the computer it's because of a fear of failure, fear of success, or fear that you aren't good enough to be a writer. This fear, or writer's block if you want to call it that, causes your brain to lock up. Ideas flee. Inspiration evaporates. The muse, if she was present, takes flight. Your muscles get tense, your breathing becomes rapid and shallow, and adrenaline kicks your central nervous system into fight-or-flight mode, which is pure instinct to get away.

If you find yourself in this type of quiet panic, bust through it by writing anything. Write down what you had for lunch that day or how you slept the night before. Write about a happy memory or a sad one. Simply start putting words on paper to get the flow started. Like an athlete stretching out prior to a big race, it will loosen you up, get the blood flowing, and move you easily into your writing project.

"I always tell myself, when I sit down to write and have a crisis of confidence, which is all writer's block is," says Erica Manfred, a freelance journalist and author, "I always say, 'that's why god invented computers. Write anything, write in any old way, don't even think about it.' You can fiddle with it later. A computer is a great invention."

The key is to get *anything* written. "Always get something on the page, even if it's crap," says freelancer Debra Gordon. "Focus on getting a rough draft down, then spend the majority of your time editing."

It may surprise you that writing just for the sake of getting words on paper doesn't necessarily mean extensive revisions later. Sophia Nash, the award-winning author of *A Dangerous Beauty*, says that she's learned that on days when she wrote anything just to get her work done for the day, later she could not distinguish the sections of her book where she had trouble from those that flowed easily. "If you force yourself, on days when you don't feel like it, to meet your page count, then afterwards, a month later when you reread the book, you will not see the portion where you didn't feel like writing. I have found that to be true," she says.

Once again, the advice about just showing up at the desk holds true. Just show up at the appointed time, sit there, and eventually something is bound to happen. Getting something down on paper is simply better than not writing anything at all. "My instincts have always been, if the creative flow isn't there, if you hang around, sooner or later it will show up," says novelist Mary Jo Putney. "If you can just write something,

> **"If I have a writing day in which the writing is more technical than emotional or inspired, at least I get some progress in the course of the plot. The next day I might go back and inject feeling."**
>
> Barbara Delinsky, *New York Times* bestselling author

you can fix it. As long as it's in your head it doesn't really exist. Get it down on paper and you've got something to work with, no matter how bad it is."

Try Editing First

If you find yourself staring at a blank page, try reviewing and revising what you wrote the day before or at your last writing session. That's how novelist Charlene Ann Baumbich begins her work each morning. "I start with editing because that's not hard for me," she says. Baumbich says that it's fun for her to see what happened in her story the day before, and this makes it easier to show up and move forward. "So when I start my day, I don't ever fear that I don't know where I'm going," she explains. "I start where I've been. Sometimes I lay down a slightly different trail, but in my mind and my story and my internal rhythm, I've worked my way back to where I left off, and I feel like I'm continuing on versus starting over every day."

Some writers do the creative work at the time that they feel most imaginative. That means that other writing-related tasks are saved for times when they aren't in peak creative form.

Novelist L.A. Banks edits in the morning because she's less creative then. "What I do is, at the top of my day, the creativity juices aren't flowing, but the hard eye editor is," she explains. "So I go back over what I wrote the night before in the cold light of day. I do a lot of hacking, cut-slash-and-burn during the morning."

Editing the previous day's work is a useful technique for getting the juices flowing. Novelist Joy Fielding is another writer who likes to revise her previous day's work before she begins the next chapter. "Anywhere from one to two hours is spent rewriting what I did the day before," she says. "The computer makes rewriting part of the process, and now I enjoy rewriting. I will redo a chapter many times as I'm doing it. It's much harder to rewrite once the book is finished."

Successful writers use a variety of approaches to capitalize on their writing schedules and generate motivation to fill blank pages. Even though every writer's process is different, they all aim to maximize time spent at their desks because it fulfills their Burning Desire to Write. Remember, successful writers write no matter what.

chapter twelve

How Professional Writers
Bust Through Writer's Block

Even though writers may stick to their schedule and show up to write at the designated time, there are some days when the words simply won't flow.

Some of the writers I interviewed believe in true writer's block, others don't. No matter which side of the fence you fall on, there will probably be days when you do everything you're supposed to do to make time to write but the words just don't flow.

This chapter reviews techniques that professional writers like Carla Neggers use to jump-start their creative flow. The techniques may seem counterintuitive, but these strategies help you get back on track if you find yourself literally at a loss for words.

Try a Change of Scenery

Sometimes the routine of showing up at the same place at the same time every day can have a negative impact on the creative process. People need variety in all areas of their lives in order to feel stimulated and enthused. If you have been writing in the same spot and looking at the same wall for a while and you're feeling your creativity wane, try switching your writing area to another location, even temporarily.

Novelist Jennifer Blake says that a change of writing scenery will often help get her creative juices flowing if she's stuck. "If the trouble is just getting started in the morning, I often change my writing place or method, leaving my office for a lounge chair before the fire in winter or the back porch in summer," she says. Blake explains that sometimes just switching back and forth between her desktop computer and a laptop or AlphaSmart, or between fountain pen and ink and a Dictaphone, will rejuvenate her creativity.

Just getting away from the desk will often cause a backlog of words or plot points to finally break free. Novelist Sandra Brown says that she often has a breakthrough in her writing when she gets up from her desk. "I'll get up and pace the room, or make a phone call, and sometimes it's several days—it can be a logjam that my mind just has to work through, and then all of a sudden, I'll be doing something else totally unrelated and I'll go, 'Ah. That's it, that's the answer.' It will suddenly unravel, then I know what I needed to do," she explains.

Take a Break

Just as a change of writing location can renew inspiration, taking a break when one is genuinely needed is an approach that successful writers use when the words aren't flowing. You may need to leave writing for the day and try again tomorrow. It's okay to walk away from your writing time if you genuinely feel that's what you need to do.

"Sometimes you reach a point in the writing where you hit the wall," says Martin Zucker, a medical and health journalist who has been writing professionally for over forty years. He suggests that when this happens your physical body and mind may need the break. "It could be that your mind is tired," he says. "Then you go meditate and recharge and your juices are flowing again. Or you knock off for the day and the next morning you're fresh again. You've got to respect and honor the source of your creativity."

Honoring the source of your creativity means that if you need to get up and go do something else, you do that. You cut yourself some slack when it's legitimate. How do you know if it's legitimate? You'll know. If you take too many breaks that are not warranted, you'll start to get that ants-in-the-pants feeling that comes from not holding yourself to your own high standards. Your Burning Desire to Write will light its flame in uncomfortable places.

If a break is truly warranted, it usually helps release the creative flow. "I learned early on that I didn't get anything done any faster sitting there like a ball and chain was around my ankle than I did going and doing other things and then coming back," says freelance writer Vicki Cobb. "Somehow the problems got solved in the interim."

Knowing when to get away from the work in progress is a central theme in successful writers' work lives. "Obviously, there are days that my brain gets stuck and I just can't find the right words or motivation to live in my head another second," says freelancer Kristina Grish. She says that when she gets to that point, she shuts her computer off and either hits the gym, reads, naps, or zones out in front of her favorite television show.

For some writers, taking a break is actually an integral part of the writing process. "I find that in the beginning, when I'm working on an idea and I have all that excitement and stuff floating around in my head, scenes and character and plot, I write for a couple of hours and then I get up and have to walk away from it," says novelist Carla Neggers. "Then I come back. So this process, this yin-yang between abandonment and concentration; concentrate for a long time, as much as I can, and then I need that abandonment to help things gel and simmer and come together."

If you truly need a break from your writing, take one. You'll return refreshed and rejuvenated.

Work on Something Different

Switching gears and working on some other writing-related task or focusing on a different section of the work in progress is another trick for getting unstuck. Tackling the book from a different perspective or working on another part of the story is an approach that novelist Rhonda Pollero will sometimes use when she's sitting at her computer, staring at a blinking cursor. "I simply start in a different way," she says. "I change the point of view, start the chapter or scene later or earlier, or ditch the scene or chapter entirely—whatever it takes to get the plot moving forward."

Writing often requires emotion, and if you were planning to write an intense scene that needs lots of energy behind it and you don't have that energy, rather than give up on writing for the day, try working on a different section of your work in progress. "Say it's a love scene, and you're just not in the mood to write a love scene," says novelist Renee Bernard. "That's fine, I'll work on something else that suits me, some dialogue, or I'll jump ahead and do a scene that comes later. I try to make as much productive use of the time as possible."

You can also switch gears by working on other tasks that are required of writers: self-promotion, Web site development, addressing and mailing out query letters, identifying markets for your work, researching agents, and studying the market to determine what editors are buying. All of these activities are legitimate uses of your time. Novelist Gemma Halliday explains that she often discovers that if she switches gears on days when she is less focused on the work in progress, she'll make up the lost pages the following day. She explains that if she allows herself to take a break now and then, "I end up getting twice as much written the next day, so it all evens out in the end."

If you are genuinely struggling with your writing one day, give yourself permission to work on something else to get the juices flowing again or work on something writing related and then strive to make up the lost work at your next writing session.

> "Writing's a solitary profession. Friends, family, and sunlight are the things that save a writers life! So if I don't feel like writing, I don't. Even when I have a deadline, if I need a break, I take it."
>
> Carly Phillips, *New York Times* bestselling author

Use an Egg Timer and Write in Short Bursts

Remember those handy dandy egg timers we've talked about before? Well, they help here too. On days when you really feel stuck but need to get in your writing (maybe you're really behind on meeting those weekly quota goals), try using an egg timer and write in multiple short bursts throughout the day.

"I frequently don't feel like writing when I'm in the middle of my first draft," says novelist Cherry Adair. "I set an egg timer in fifteen-minute increments. Write for fifteen minutes. Pull weeds for fifteen minutes (or whatever I feel like doing that's away from my computer) and then come back and do it again. And again and again!"

This is a great way to get in some writing if you are feeling like you're simply avoiding your work.

Sweat It Out

A surprising caveat that many aspiring writers may not be aware of: sitting at a computer for long periods of time on a routine basis takes its toll on your body. Writing requires not only mental stamina but physical stamina too. If you aren't used to sitting for extended periods of time (like you do in the Blitz schedule, for instance), your backside will likely be numb, your shoulders tight, and your neck stiff. To combat this, most writers say that exercise is a critical part of their day. They use it to jump-start their brains, keep their minds fresh, and work out the kinks not only in their writing but in their backs as well.

> "If I'm in a pattern of avoidance, I'll set the timer and write in twenty-minute segments."
>
> Barbara Samuel, award-winning romance author

"I regard myself as a writing athlete," says freelancer Martin Zucker. He does yoga every day as part of his work routine.

Freelance writer Christie Taylor explains that regular exercise is a part of her work routine, because not only does it help get her energy flowing, it reinforces the self-discipline that is inherent to success as a writer. "Maybe it's because I danced from such a young age, and there was a discipline to that that really helped me," she says. "I find that when I exercise, some of that comes back."

Exercise also stimulates the creative process; it's similar to taking a break in that it often loosens up mental logjams in the mind. Freelancer Cecil Murphey uses regular exercise as a way to think through his writing. He says that he does much of the processing in his head when he's jogging.

Exercise is an excellent way to rejuvenate your creativity. Not only will it help you regain your creative edge, you'll be doing something great for your body too.

Take a Nap

Fatigue, either mental or physical, is not conducive to writing, and it's definitely a factor to take into consideration if you are working full time, caring for children, or simply trying to live your life and get your writing done as well. Writing is usually the first victim of the "I'm too tired" dilemma that can come from attending to all our lower-level needs on Maslow's hierarchy. And the creative process itself can sometimes be exhausting; it takes more mental energy than we often realize.

One solution is to take a short twenty-minute nap when you feel too tired to write. The benefits of short naps have been documented consistently. In one study in Japan, a group of healthy adults took a twenty-minute nap or a twenty-minute rest one hour after performing two hours of visual work, followed by another hour of work.

Researchers discovered that the twenty-minute rest temporarily alleviated the person's sleepiness, but drowsiness returned during the additional one hour of work. However, those who took a twenty-minute nap maintained alertness, performed at higher levels, and reported lower levels of mental fatigue during the additional one-hour work period. These results suggest that a short nap is useful for both fatigue prevention and recovery during continuous periods of work.

Journal

Since writers love words and love getting their own thoughts down on paper, journaling is often a secret pleasure and a hidden joy. Something about that connection between hand, pen, arm, and heart feels luscious. Keeping a journal can seem practically decadent in these time-strapped days, but using a journal is one strategy that some writers employ to get their creative juices flowing.

For instance, freelance writer and author Tara Dillard keeps a word journal. When she's stuck, or if she needs an interesting or unusual jumping off point for the day, she opens up her journal, picks out several words or phrases, and begins. "I just open it up and see four words that I like," she says. "It perks up my writing because I'm using those four words. I don't know how, but I'm using those four words."

Dillard also keeps a journal of unique phrases that catch her eye, and she files quotes that appeal to her for future reference. Whenever her writing needs a booster shot, she turns to her journals for inspiration.

chapter thirteen

The Inner Critic and Other Goblins

You've chosen a schedule and are working it diligently. You've set writing goals and made your Writing Action Plan. These are all critical strategies that provide a solid foundation for managing day-to-day activities while also finding time to write and making writing part of your lifestyle.

Even with these solid techniques in place, there may be internal obstacles that keep you from making time to write. For instance, every writer has his or her own internal critic, and some days its voice is harsh, loud, and distracting. Even successful writers sometimes feel discouraged about the writing process. Aspiring writers can feel discouraged about how long it takes to get published. In this chapter, we'll look at the issues that cause a writer to stop writing and review the strategies that authors like Susan Grant use to overcome them.

When You Are Your Own Worst Critic

The harsh voice of an internal critic is a dilemma that all writers face. That critic can keep you from forging ahead with your writing aspirations—if you let it. It can sidetrack you and convince you not to get your writing done that day. Who wants to hear what you have to say anyway, it tells you. Aspiring writers aren't alone with this problem. Let's look at how successful writers deal with their internal critics.

Ignore It

All of us must deal with our personal saboteurs that discourage us from making time to write. One strategy that many professional writers use is to simply ignore it and keep writing.

"It's like there's a goblin sitting on each shoulder: the Goblin of Stupid and the other is the Goblin of Boring," says novelist Susan Grant. "Periodically they blurt out, 'That's stupid!' and I'll keep writing, and the other one blurts out, 'That's boring!' So boring, stupid, stupid, boring. And I've got to put ear plugs in and try not to listen to them and just write."

Let the Critic Write First

If your internal critic is particularly disruptive one day, give it a pen and let it write. I've heard this referred to as "vomiting on the page." Not literally, of course. What you do is take out a few blank pieces of paper and let your critic go wild. Let it write anything it wants to, like that you're not good enough to be a writer, that you're selfish for taking this hour away from your family, that nobody wants to hear what you have to say, or whatever. Just let it rip. After awhile it winds down, and you can then move to your work in progress without that negative running commentary from the peanut gallery. "Let it write everything and then it'll quit, because it's lazy," says novelist Ann Major. "That's a trick that will work."

After you're done, go a step further and shred or rip up those pages and throw them in the wastebasket. Visualize that you're tossing your inner critic aside. This exercise will help clear your mind so that you can then get to work.

The Power of Positive Thinking

Motivational leaders like Norman Vincent Peale, Napoleon Hill, and many others have spoken about the benefits of using positive messages to advance toward one's goals. Positive thinking for writers is a useful strategy for maintaining or regaining focus on days when the internal critic is loud. Remember your Vision of Success? Positive messages help to reinforce it because you're telling yourself that, yes, you can get there.

Positive messages for writers are short, one-sentence esteem boosters. Examples of positive messages for writers include statements like, "I can do this," "If I persevere, I will find success as a writer," and "My writing is getting better every day." Any statement that serves to motivate you to continue with your writing will work. It's a good idea to create two or three positive messages for yourself, then read them aloud when the going gets tough.

Many years ago, I created a small, hand-written statement that reads, "You can do it." I put it in a pretty picture frame beside my computer. I still have it. It's a constant motivator to keep going.

Many successful writers have used this approach. Novelist Robyn Carr says that for her, voicing positives about her writing helps her stay focused, on task, and moving forward. "Over time, I've become very good at putting positive spins on things, seeing that everything works out the way it's supposed to, almost always for the best," she says. "I find the advantage in setbacks, reasoning how things could turn to my favor."

That's an advantageous mindset for writers to develop, because we all know that to become successful is going to take time, lots of perseverance, and the weathering of rejection and discouragement. To that end, Carr goes on to explain how she uses positive messages to motivate herself to keep writing. "I spend a lot of time consciously practicing the power of positive thinking, writing down my goals and affirmations, visualizing success, and reading positive self-help books. And even more importantly, I remind myself constantly to work on those things I can control—and it usually comes down to writing more good books. I can't control the size of the print runs, the reviews, the publisher's enthusiasm, or word-of-mouth popularity. But I can do my best at the storytelling, constantly striving to do a better job."

> **"If you can preserve the joy of writing, I think your voice will come through more strongly, and your book will be better."**
>
> Eloisa James, *New York Times* and *USA Today* bestselling author

Sticking to positive messages and using positive self-talk is how David Groves, a book author and freelance writer, managed an interview with Barry Goldwater, Sr. in 1985 at the beginning of his fledgling writing career. Groves was thirty years old at the time and not a political writer. He'd gotten the assignment from an in-flight magazine based on some previous work he'd done for them. He accepted the assignment, but he was nervous. This wasn't his area of expertise, and he was still relatively new as a writer. The magazine flew him to Washington, D.C., to interview the senator. Groves says he got through it by using lots of positive self-talk. He kept telling himself, "There are other people who do this at this age, why can't I do this? What makes them so much better than me?"

How did the interview go? "It went great," says Groves. "They only gave me fifteen minutes, but I had questions in case it went long. He liked me, and he got into a groove, and after forty-five minutes, his secretary came in and said, 'The Armed Services Committee is waiting.' And he said, 'Let them wait.' So I got fifty-five minutes out of it, and it was a great story."

Groves is a perfect example of how using positive self-talk can get you through stressful and unknown situations and how you can take some leaps in your own writing career that you may have previously been afraid of doing. Have you been sitting on a manuscript that you really want to get published but feel fearful that no agent will look at it? Are you afraid to step out and send query letters to major magazines for fear that you're not good enough to break in?

Remember, all you need is one good idea. Tell yourself that you can do it, that you are good enough, and that you deserve to have your Vision of Success come to fruition. Actively dispute the critic through the use of positive messages. Pat yourself on the back for working toward your dream of becoming a professional writer. Create your own positive messages and tape them on the wall next to the computer. When the internal critic is harsh, read the messages out loud and return to your work.

Psychology 101: *Acting As If*

Sticking to positive messages, the foundation of our next strategy, is known in psychology as *Acting as if*. Around the turn of the twentieth century, a researcher named Alfred Adler studied social psychology and postulated that humans are social creatures who form conclusions about themselves by observing their own behavior, much as they draw conclusions of other people by observing them.

From that theory sprang the practical exercise of *Acting as if*. The thinking behind it is that if you *Act as if* you already are whatever it is you want to be, eventually you begin to feel that you are what you are pretending to be. Subsequently, you start behaving in ways that will actually bring that state about. In other words, you become what you are practicing. This is why positive messages, or affirmations as some people call them, are written in the present tense, as if that condition already exists. It's also why your Vision of Success is so critical. *Acting as if* requires an end goal. Your success as a writer (in whatever form your long-term goal is written) is your destination, and *Acting as if* is one tool for reaching that destination.

You can also think of it this way: how you think is how you feel. Change your thoughts and you'll change your feelings, which will in turn impact your behavior. Start out by thinking "I'm a successful writer" as often as possible. This will reinforce the Vision of Success that you've been holding like a virtual photograph in the forefront of your mind. The more you practice *Acting as if* you are already a successful writer, the more you will feel that you are, which in turn will influence how you behave and motivate you to take action.

Actions bring about results, but behind every action is a solid, goal-driven thought. Remember: all human behavior is goal directed. An intention to meet the goal arises—for example, your nose itches, and your intention becomes to stop the itching. You raise your hand to your nose to scratch it with the intention of stopping that itch. But before you raised your hand to your nose, there was a thought behind that action that generated the intention, even if you're not conscious of it. The thought/intention was, "I'm going to raise my hand to my nose so that I can scratch it and stop the itch." The goal was to stop the itch.

It's the same thing with writing: you want to be a successful writer, so you want to make time to write. Before you can take action to make time to write, you've got to have the thought/intention to generate the action. So tell yourself the thoughts that will get you to your desk. A good place to start is to use your Writing Action Plan. The goals you listed there are essentially your intentions. This is why I wanted you to post the plan in a prominent location as well as read it out loud every day. Reciting those goals to yourself influences your behavior and generates action.

Novelist Tara Taylor Quinn gives us an example of how she used the strategy of practicing being a confident, successful writer in her own writing life several years before she got published. Notice how this strategy impacted those around her—*Acting as if* is another good way to enlist your family's support. "I had to believe that writing, whether published or not, was something deserving of respect, both from myself and from those around me who didn't take it seriously. Once I respected myself and what I was doing, once I took me seriously, I started to act accordingly and those around me eventually came around," she says.

Write Anyway

Instead of succumbing to the fight-or-flight panic that sets in when feeling blocked or overwhelmed with writing, professional writers take the opposite approach and simply carry on. Writing becomes the salve that calms the struggle.

Positive self-talk and drawing on the quiet confidence that years of consistent work produces is what gets novelist Sandra Brown through the times of lost focus. "I keep telling myself, on a hard day when it's just not coming, it's just not there, 'I've done this sixty-eight times. I know how to do this. Just take a deep breath, hang in there, and it'll eventually shake loose.' Because I know it's in my head, it's just getting it from there to my fingertips," she says.

Striving to move forward in the current novel is key to helping novelist Carla Neggers through the occasional setbacks. "The key is I've always kept writing. Whatever setbacks there were or whatever was going on up or down, I always focus on the work in progress. There's always the next book, whether things are going well or not going well. You can't succeed as a writer if you don't write," she says.

Novelist Robyn Carr reiterates the advice that writing through any periods of discouragement is critical, and she adds that there's often an unexpected yet pleasant payoff to the practice. "When I struggle with the actual writing, it often opens up a new avenue, a better direction, an opportunity for a course correction, a chance to reinvent myself," she says. "For example, I had a very successful thriller years ago, and I tried desperately to write another one—but the writing came very hard, the attempts were rejected. I just wasn't scary or edgy enough for suspense. Finally I stopped trying to fit a square peg in a round hole and returned to my women's fiction roots, concentrating on what I was actually best at—characterization, relationships, women's issues."

Coping with the Discouragement Goblin

Successful writers write because they love words, books, and reading. They want to see their own words on paper; however, the writers I interviewed said that even if they never got published again, they'd keep writing.

"In my case, being discouraged hasn't meant that I've had to get back on track because it hasn't meant that I've stopped," says novelist Kathryn Harrison. "I am, as I said, addicted to it—when I'm not writing I'm anxious, agitated, and unhappy. So even doing work that I'm not happy with is better than that; it means I'm moving toward improving it."As mentioned in Chapter 2, many writers feel that writing is so much a part of them that they don't require an outside motivator to do it. You probably don't either. Writers write. Writing is something you have to do, and you are driven to find the time to do it despite your busy life.

"I love to write. I love to create and get lost in the writing. If I never sold another book, I would still write. I would likely stop submitting to publishers somewhere along the way, but I don't need an incentive to write," says award-winning novelist Linda Winstead Jones, author of *Prince of Magic* and *Prince of Fire*.

The abiding love of writing itself sustains writers through any difficult periods. "I have to write," says novelist Tara Taylor Quinn. "It's not an option. I understand this about myself and so it happens. If I'm not writing, I'm not emotionally or mentally in sync with myself. Molehills become mountains. I get irritable. I don't find joy in things that normally bring me pleasure. I know that when I feel that way, I have to get to my desk and write."

Writing is that important to writers. "If I didn't keep writing I would lose my sanity," says freelancer Daphne Kalotay, "knowing all the things I mean to write but haven't."

Freelancer Alix Strauss cherishes the variety of work that writing offers her, as well as the fact that she has made a mark on the world. "Every day is different," she says. "If I drop dead tomorrow, I've made an impact. My work is out there, you can't erase that. You can't take away a book."

Work with a Partner

Cultivating friends or other aspiring writers who can be supportive about your work is another strategy that successful writers have used to overcome internal obstacles that prevent them from making time to write. (See Chapter 17 for more on this.) Finding a critique buddy who can be truthful but kind helps motivate you to write and encourages you to stick to those positive messages. It can also give you another perspective on your own work—what you thought sucked might actually be pretty good, while something you thought was okay might need improvement. A trusted writing partner can be a huge asset to your development as a writer.

Working with a partner is also a great way to reinforce your writing schedule and hold yourself accountable to getting your work done, especially when you set a joint timeline and agree to submit your work to each other by a certain date. Comedy writer Lynne Alpern teamed up with another aspiring writer in the beginning of her career. The women made a commitment to a joint project in order to hold themselves accountable. "Having a partner helped both of us keep going, it was someone we had to answer to," Alpern says. "If I said I'm going to work on X, I better get it accomplished. It's so easy to procrastinate if you're by yourself."

Alpern adds that she and her partner also had opportunities to learn together instead of alone since they were both newbies at the time and groping their way along. It was a strategy that worked; Alpern and her writing partner had a twenty-year association and wrote hundreds of articles together. "I think part of our success was working together at a time when we were both feeling our way along and pursuing it from different angles," she says.

Working with a partner has the added benefit of providing a sounding board for ideas. Partnership is key for married writing team Joyce and Jim Lavene. "Having each other to talk over stories, go to book events, come up with new ideas, laugh about the problems, whine and complain when things don't go our way; it's great having a good friend in the business that lives and works with you," they say.

> "You can't worry about creating the masterpiece. It'll paralyze you, thinking that every word has to be golden. It doesn't work like that. You just keep going."
>
> Vicki Cobb, freelance writer

If you find that lack of focus is a trend for you, enlist the support of another aspiring writer to keep you on track. Begin a joint writing project that requires both writers to submit work to each other by an agreed upon date. Or plan to meet at the library to research, edit, or write together.

Only You Can Get You to the Desk

As you've probably noticed, developing and exercising liberal doses of self-discipline is a prominent theme that supports many successful writers' work habits. What it boils down to is that only you can get yourself to the desk. There's really no way to do this other than to make yourself follow through. Remember, self-discipline is like a muscle; the more you use it, the stronger it gets.

Novelist Rick Mofina says he often had conversations with himself in the early days of his career when he was tired and preferred to sleep in rather than get up and work his Early - Morning schedule, but the fact that only he could get his writing done got him up. "I would lay there thinking, 'Okay, I had a hard week,' and maybe I even traveled on assignment for a couple of days, and I deserve the day off," he says. "Then my other self would say, as boss, 'You're fired, because there's a keyboard waiting for you and the job's not getting done. So you can lay here and pretend you're writing a book and not get it done, while the other Rick is at the keyboard, getting the job done.' And that's what separates the people that are in bookstores from those who dream about being in bookstores."

Writers are creative high achievers, and creative high achievers are highly disciplined people. They have

> **"It's easy to get distracted if you're looking for distractions. What I try to do is focus on my priorities and understand what they are, and commit to them. So for me, writing is a priority and I commit to that, then distractions are less tempting."**
>
> Carla Neggers, *New York Times* bestselling author

learned to make time to write no matter what else is going on at home or in their lives. With obvious exceptions for major life events or emergencies, professional writers enforce their own rules about their writing schedules and meeting their short-term-quota goals.

"You must finish what you begin," says novelist Catherine Coulter. "You must be a closer. You must write the same number of hours every day. You must set a number of pages you will write each day."

Perseverance Will Pay Off

Professional writers persevere because they know that the self-discipline they exercise today pays off big in the future. Sometimes, extraordinary perseverance is required early on in the beginning of a writing career. "I rewrote my first book (*Magnificent Passage*) thirty-two times front to back," says novelist Kat Martin. "I'd learn something new and I'd change it. I just kept it up and eventually it was good enough to sell at that point." Martin adds that even though she often felt discouraged, she kept writing, and by the time her first book sold she'd written two more. That's one benefit of developing self-discipline: it fuels the motivation to keep going even in the face of rejection, which is something that all writers will face.

The bottom line is successful writers don't let anything get in the way of getting their work done. Novelist Sandra Marton once wrote in her car when there was a power outage in her neighborhood. She plugged her portable computer into the car's cigarette lighter.

Stephen Fenichell, a freelance writer and book author, says that for him, persevering has meant staying focused and learning to compartmentalize writing time in order to keep it distraction free. "I try to do the business things in the morning and save the afternoons for hitting the keyboard," he says. "I think keeping those things divided is useful." Begin to exercise self-discipline in your own life when it comes to writing. Post your schedule, work your Writing Action Plan, and consistently strive to meet your writing goals. Remember, you're the only one who can get the job done.

Cultivate Persistence

As an aspiring writer, you know that persistence will be demanded of you as you journey forward on your path to success. Rejection is a writer's lot, and an attitude of persistence will also help you stay focused on your writing goals. The easiest way to develop persistence is by exercising self-discipline and following your writing schedule. Keeping your eye on the end goal and holding your Vision of Success firmly in mind will also help.

Persistence is a good trait to have as a writer, because when one book or article is finished, the next one is yet to be written. You finish one project and then there you are, staring at the blank page again. "Let me tell you—the only way to write a book is to put words on paper, and whether you're a bestselling author who's got thousands of readers, or whether you're writing your first book, you can still put only one word on the page at a time," says novelist Sandra Brown. "That's the only way I know how to do it, is to keep your butt in the chair and put words on paper."

Successful writers keep writing because they love it. "It's an incredibly powerful and rewarding job, and anybody who has the opportunity to do it should treasure it," says freelancer Tim O'Shei. "And I love it. I love to tell a good story, so why would I ever give it up?"

Successful writers use a variety of techniques to stay focused on their writing, nurture their Burning Desire to Write, and make progress on their current projects. They make time to write over and over again because they love it so much.

chapter fourteen

Got Distractions?

*F*or many of the professional writers I interviewed, making time to write means they work from home because that's the most natural way to fit writing into their lifestyles. Because of that, they've learned to recognize and manage the inevitable distractions that writing at home creates. There are distractions created by people: children, spouses, drop-in neighbors, maintenance workers, and package deliveries (often for neighbors who are away at regular jobs). There are distractions like the pile of laundry in the corner that begs for attention. And sneaky distractions like surfing the Internet, checking e-mail, and taking telephone calls can chew up hours of precious writing time.

Successful writers, like bestselling author Sabrina Jeffries, have developed creative, commonsense, and reliable strategies for coping with all of these distractions. These strategies allow them to follow their writing schedules while juggling their other responsibilities.

Once Again, Post Your Writing Schedule

The biggest distraction from writing cited by successful writers who work at home is other people: family, friends, neighbors, children, or the UPS delivery guy. The previous strategies that help with balancing family life and writing also help in the arena of dealing with the interruptions that those family members and other people can create.

One key approach is to capitalize on the writing schedule that you've been working by hanging it up somewhere visible to everyone: on the door to the space you're working in, the refrigerator, or next to the family calendar. Posting your writing schedule serves to reinforce to everyone that when you are writing, you're working. It helps them understand that during that time you are not to be disturbed unless there is an emergency. It will help your family and everyone else learn to support, honor, and respect your writing time (or, at the very least, to leave you alone while you write).

Novelist Christine Feehan explains that relying on that familial support, plus the discipline of writing on a set schedule that she's cultivated over the years, has been an important element for managing distractions at home while she's working. "I believe in laying it out to my family that these are my working hours, and that unless there is something extraordinary, do not interrupt me," she says. "I close the door. The only one who's allowed ever to interrupt me for any reason other than an emergency is my sixteen-year-old. But everybody else, they get to wait. It is a matter of discipline, and it's a matter of disciplining your family to understand that you're doing a job."

When family or other distractions threaten to pull you away from your desk, it's your posted writing schedule that will help you stay seated. Not only can you look at it and see that this is your writing time, but you can point out to the interrupter that this is your time to write and that whatever they are asking of you will have to wait.

"I do occasionally have to tell family members that I have a job and am not always available," says novelist Linda Winstead Jones, "even though I'm home and it looks to them as if I am available. I had to learn to say no early on."

Psychology 101: A Short Lesson on Reinforcement

How do you alter the behavior of people interrupting you while you're writing? Post your writing schedule, and then refuse to get up *every single time* you are interrupted (barring a true emergency, of course). Never answer the phone, the doorbell, respond to e-mail, and so forth while you're writing.

This is how you'll teach people in your environment not to knock on the door or call or e-mail when you're writing, because if you never get up, they don't get reinforced for interrupting. If you stop writing *every now and then* to take a phone call or clean up spilled milk or sign for a UPS delivery for your neighbor, that's called intermittent reinforcement and it is the strongest type of reinforcement that exists. It increases the very behavior you are attempting to extinguish. You're actually reinforcing the interrupting behavior and increasing the chances that it will happen again.

If your spouse knocks on your office door fifteen times a day, and you hold out for two days but on the third day and the sixteenth time he knocks you finally get exasperated enough to get up and answer it, he has hit the jackpot. You've reinforced that behavior and significantly increased the chance that it will happen again.

So yes, it's hard, but practice not getting up when they knock, every single time, and eventually you will *extinguish* the interrupting behavior. Then when they do interrupt, you'll know it's because it is truly something that can't wait.

Life Happens

In reality, there may be times when you have to stop writing to tend to something within your home or with your family. That's okay; life happens. Learn to be flexible. Being able to move from writing to a task that needs tending to and back to writing again is a key strategy successful writers use to ensure that they meet the needs of their families and also make progress in their writing careers. Novelist Wendy Corsi Staub has learned to adjust her writing schedule around inevitable interruptions that being a mom creates. Staub explains that if she has to stop working due to a more pressing family need, she simply makes up the lost time later. This is the nice thing about quota goals—if you don't meet them one day, you can simply make them up at the next writing session.

"I have been able to chaperone all of my children's field trips, read to their classes, pick them up when the school nurse calls midday. Yes, those are distractions, but I take them in stride and adjust my schedule accordingly," says Staub. "A sick child or family member is by far the biggest setback I have ever encountered. Of course, I can't anticipate when I'll have to drop everything and run someone to the pediatrician, then spend sleepless nights on bedside duty. All I can do later is make up for the lost time by working twice as long after things have righted themselves."

Author Steve Berry has learned to simply incorporate the many distractions he faces every day as he writes and continues his law practice. He adjusts his writing to accommodate the interruptions rather than trying to avoid, limit, or extinguish them. He explains that by learning how to go with the flow of events and moving smoothly from writing to the task that needs tending to and back to the writing again is a critical element for his success. "I'll write a little bit, [my staff] say it's time to go do something, I go do it and come back and pick up where I left off. I've never had the luxury of just being able to sit here and say okay, I'm here, and nobody bother me and let me create. It doesn't work like that," he says. "I have to earn a living and pay the bills. You've got to adapt the writing into your day."

Berry's comment hearkens back to Chapter 4 and writing schedules. If your lifestyle is one that comes with many distractions—perhaps you have very small children, or you write at work like Berry does—you may have to choose the Any-Opportunity writing schedule or the Miniblocks-of-time schedule to get your work done. Distractions will exist at every point in your writing career. In those instances, adapt your creative flow to the interruptions and learn to switch gears easily and frequently.

The Major Time Zappers: Internet, E-Mail, and Telephone

Sometimes a writer's distractions don't come from the pitter-patter of little feet or a neighbor who wants to go see a movie in the middle of the day. Sometimes the distractions are right there in front of him, in the same room, and on his computer. Receiving phone calls, surfing the Internet, and checking e-mail are huge time wasters for professional writers, and many struggle to avoid these tempting side roads. Some writers go to extraordinary lengths to ensure that these demons don't steal their writing time.

The primary thing to do is, once again, exercise self-discipline. If you get sucked into Internet surfing or composing lengthy e-mails to all your friends and family, don't allow yourself to even open the programs until you're done writing for the day. "You have to recognize that if you go to certain places on the Internet and that shuts you down, don't do it," says novelist Susan Grant. "What I've been doing during my writing time is going up to the actual cable box and pulling it out of the wall so that I'm not tempted. I'm just trying to take away the temptation. You've just got to do it."

If the phone is your Achilles heel, turn off the ringer or get caller ID so you can ignore sales reps or calls from chatty friends. Novelist Merline Lovelace even went so far as to move the answering machine into another room so that she wouldn't be tempted to pick up when she hears who's calling. "My writing time is my writing time," she says. "I don't answer the phone, I don't answer the door."

The Internet is another huge time waster for many people. This is a tricky one, because researching material on the Internet is part of life as a writer. One strategy that novelist Barbara Samuel has used to combat falling into the black hole of Internet surfing is to not have her writing computer connected to the World Wide Web. "My biggest challenge is the Internet, because it feels like I'm writing," she says. "The same parts of my brain are satisfied by e-mail, blogs, et cetera. To counter that, I keep e-mail off my writing computer, and the Internet computer is in another room."

With e-mail, close the program while you're writing. If you hate not responding to people, set up your e-mail software to automatically respond to people who send you e-mail. That way the sender gets a response, and you can send a more personalized one when you're done writing.

"Do use that technology to put some parameters around your space, because your space is where you create," says novelist L.A. Banks.

When You're Writing, You're Working

A key strategy for success when managing distractions is to adopt, and then project out, an attitude of writing equals working. You should already be treating your writing like a job. This approach comes in handy here too. Treating writing time seriously and approaching it like a job are useful self-disciplinary measures that help manage distractions when you're writing from home.

Tinker Ready is a freelance writer who started her career as a daily newspaper reporter. That was good training on how to write, she says, but when she started working from home after her son was born, she struggled with distractions. What worked for her was cultivating a mindset of when she's sitting at her desk at home, she's working. "That was very hard to do, saying no to people when they came over," she says. "People think you're not working if you work at home. So if somebody calls up and wants to do something, I say, 'It's a work day for me.'"

Plan For Distractions ahead of Time

Another strategy for success when dealing with distractions is to plan for those distractions that you know will occur and construct your writing time around those. In other words, plan your work and work your plan. This is where your writing schedule will again help you find time to write. This is why you have a writing schedule to begin with. You want to design your day around your writing as much as possible. Remember, time to write is one of your basic needs in Maslow's hierarchy that your schedule accommodates. Writing is the big rock that you want to put in the jar first. Your other tasks will slip in around it. So when you make your schedule for the week, pencil in writing first, then add the must-do tasks of day-to-day life.

While it's impossible to plan for every conceivable distraction, scheduling writing time first and filling your day with your other obligations will lessen your stress levels because you're more likely to get your writing done, which in turn will help you feel more in control of your own time. "At the beginning of each week, and each day, I look at what I have to do that week including who is going to need what from me, and I slot times for all of it," says novelist Tara Taylor Quinn. "That not only sets a plan, it shows me a picture of the possibilities. It shows me it can be done, and it also frees my mind up to not have to worry about what's out there pushing at me. I have it all down, managed, and then I can relax and just do it."

Marie Bostwick, the award-winning author of *River's Edge* and *Fields of Gold*, takes her son to school every morning and cares for an elderly parent. But by planning for these other obligations ahead of time, she is able to spend quality time with her child, meet the demands of running a household, and accomplish her writing goals for the day. "You've got to figure all that in there," she says. "But when I sit down to write, that's it."

Planning even the smallest details of the day, such as grocery shopping, is the trick that successful writers use. Novelist Robyn Carr adopts a blitz-and-delegate strategy to complete all errands and other household obligations that might distract her from her writing, everything from house cleaning and grocery shopping to buying birthday cards. "I have learned to do these things fast," she says. "And I delegate. I can whip through a house in an hour, I pay bills online, if I have to shop for Christmas or birthdays, I set aside a few hours at a mall and go for it! When I buy a birthday card, I buy ten; I always get several printer cartridges, envelopes, and stamps at a time. I keep a note pad in the kitchen, and if you don't write down a food item you used up or would like to have, it won't get picked up at the store. He who is already out (kid on his way home from school or football, husband on his way home from work) can stop and pick up cleaning, dinner, et cetera."

> **"My laptop is a virgin. It will never be hooked up to e-mail."**
>
> Sophia Nash, award-winning author of
> *A Dangerous Beauty*

Another way to plan for distractions is to allot time for those activities that you know will crop up. Freelance writer Georgia Richardson handles her writing and household responsibilities this way. "The first thing I did was purchase two timers—one for domestic chores, the other for writing," she says. "I have a certain amount of time set aside for both, and if necessary, I can rearrange my time—for instance, when unexpected company arrives, or I have a deadline looming and need more writing time."

If distractions are a major obstacle for you that prevent you from writing, try this: for one week, make a list of the distractions that tempt you away from your scheduled writing time. Then brainstorm ways you can overcome those distractions. If your family or children have needs that you know will come up, schedule time to meet those that is separate from your scheduled writing time. Set aside one day to run all your errands for the upcoming week. And be tough with yourself so that when you sit down to write, you write.

Use Distractions as a Reward for Writing

Since most writers are creative high achievers who have a broad array of interests, why not use a distraction that lures you away from writing to begin with as a reward for writing? If you like to paint, shop, or go in-line skating, reward yourself with that activity once you get your writing done.

Novelist Jennifer Blake says that in addition to writing she likes to travel, garden, paint, quilt, knit, bead, make jewelry, and shop at flea markets and antique shops. Her solution is to reward herself with one of those activities after she gets her writing done. "The interest of the moment becomes my reward for getting my writing stint done for the day or the week," she explains. "It's all a matter of balance; a writer's world can become too focused on mental effort. I'm a better writer, or so I like to think, for allowing myself outside interests."

You want to associate positive feelings with the self-discipline you've been exercising; rewarding yourself for meeting goals increases the chances that you'll keep going with it. You won't feel motivated to write if it's only a grueling chore for you. So work your writing schedule, then pat yourself on the back for following through and go skating with your kids.

When Ideas Are a Distraction

Professional writers often have many ideas floating around their brains at any given time. Sometimes their own creativity can be a distraction that lures them away from their current project.

Novelist Renee Bernard says that she made the mistake of starting a new book while writing the current one, and then found herself making very little progress on two books. What she did was start keeping an idea file so she could focus on the book at hand. "I have a file folder with future ideas," she says, "and I write down a fragment and I file it away. If it's good, it'll be good later."

If ideas are whirling around in your mind and distracting you from making forward progress on your current writing project, purchase a spiral notebook that you carry with you at all times to jot down your thoughts and ideas, and then return your focus to your current piece.

Remove Yourself from the Distractions

Working from home in any endeavor means there will be interruptions that can intrude on your work time, no matter how diligent you are about protecting it. One strategy that some writers have used is to acquire alternate work space. Novelist Sandra Brown decided to rent an office because the distractions at her home office became too frequent. "I was the depot for FedEx and UPS," she says. Brown adds that another benefit to having a writing space that was separate from her home was that it helped her make the transition from writing back to her family life in the evening. "When I went to work—it was a block and a half to a little strip center that had office space—I could go to work," she says. "It took me ninety seconds to get there, but that's what I did when I was there. I couldn't fold laundry, I couldn't put on a pot roast, I couldn't do anything else. Then, when I went home, just that separation from it, home was special again. Home meant rest, relax, visit with your kids, talk to your husband. So that worked for me."

If renting office space is not economically feasible for you at this time, how about writing at a coffee shop? That's what novelist Sabrina Jeffries did. "I get very distracted at home, so I find it easier to go to a coffee house to write. I can go into hyperfocus when there's lots of noise around. At home it's just too quiet. And also there are too many other things I need to do at home, so I get to the end of the day and I find that I have done plenty of little stuff around the house but I haven't written any," she says.

Since novelist Roxanne St. Claire prefers a quieter environment in which to work, she says that in the summer, when her children are out of school, she'll often take a laptop to the library for a few hours every day and write.

Freelance writer Rachel Safier, author of *Mr. Right Now* and *Boy Meets Girl*, often works at a neighbor's house to eliminate distractions. "I've found success in packing up my laptop and my dog several days a week and going to work across the street in a friend's kitchen while she's away at the office," she says. "Her dog and mine entertain each other, and in someone else's space, where the laundry that needs to be done isn't mine and the food in the fridge isn't mine, I'm less tempted to putter about."

Psychology 101: Maybe It's Just Resistance

One of the key distinctions writers need to learn to make is between a true distraction and when you are simply resisting getting to your desk. A true distraction is one that demands your attention at the moment, one that you cannot let go by—a sick child or pet, a truly urgent phone call, your own illness, a broken water pipe inside the house, or some other unexpected situation that genuinely pulls you away from your work.

Resistance is a tempting but totally unnecessary task that lures you away from writing—the laundry, for instance. Unless your household is faced with going naked, that pile of dirty clothes can wait until you draft your article idea or write your three pages. Resistance to writing manipulates you into allowing those general distractions to interfere with your work. You have an hour of writing scheduled, but instead you find yourself standing in a steamy laundry room debating whether to use powdered or liquid detergent.

When you make the commitment to establish a career as a writer, recognition of this resistance is a key to success. You must learn to see your own self-sabotaging actions and immediately counter them.

An effective way to overcome resistance is to utilize a pre-planned replacement thought. A replacement thought is your argument to the resistance and how you mentally arm yourself against all the ways you sabotage your own future.

Using replacement thoughts for dealing with resistance is a proven strategy. It takes time and practice because your old thought patterns have worn grooves into your brain, and you have to feed yourself new thoughts in order to create new grooves. With practice, the new grooves will begin to form and you will find your resistance decreasing. But don't expect resistance to go away completely, because it probably won't. Resistance to doing what is good for us is part of the human condition. What's important is that you manage it, or else it will manage you.

Use the following worksheet to identify your resistance thoughts and create new, more productive thoughts to combat them. I've started you off with an example.

Worksheet: How to Master Resistance

There are four parts to this exercise. First, think back to the last time you wanted to write and didn't. What were you doing at the time? Where were you? What else was going on in the environment or your life at the time? What thoughts went through your head that prevented you from writing? Then list two other times that resistance occurred, taking careful note of any patterns that arise. Identify the resistance thoughts that came to mind that prevented you from following through on your writing. Last, create replacement thoughts to use in the future. In each section, I give you an example to help get you started.

Identifying Resistance Thoughts: *Example*

Date and time I wanted to or had scheduled to write but didn't: *last Friday from two to three p.m.*

I was doing *housecleaning* instead.

Where I was: *home*

What else was going on at the time: *the kids were finger painting upstairs and the dog had an appointment with the vet later that afternoon, plus the in-laws were coming for dinner*

Thoughts going through my head that kept me from writing: *there's not enough time, there's too much going on right now, I've got too much to do, I can't write when the kids are here*

Identifying Resistance Thoughts

Date and time I wanted to or had scheduled to write
but didn't: _____

I was doing _____ instead.

Where I was: _____

What else was going on at the time: _____

_____

_____

_____

_____

_____

Thoughts going through my head that kept me from
writing: _____

_____

_____

_____

_____

_____

Now think back to two additional times that you wanted to
write and you didn't. Again, identify what you were doing at the
time, where you were, and what else was going on:

Identifying Resistance Thoughts (continued)

Last two dates and times I wanted to or had scheduled
to write: _____

I was doing _____ and
_____ instead.

Where I was: _____ and
_____

What else was going on at the time: _____
_____
_____
_____
_____
_____
_____

Thoughts going through my head that kept me from
writing: _____
_____
_____
_____
_____
_____
_____

Now compile from your work above the prominent
thoughts that went through your head that kept you
from writing. Notice any themes or similarities.

Resistance Themes

There are too many other obligations right now.

Or:

I can't write when others are in the house, it's too noisy.

Or:

I have too many other things to do right now.

Your turn: _____

_____

_____

_____

_____

_____

_____

_____

_____

_____

_____

_____

_____

_____

Last, create action-oriented replacement thoughts. For each resistance thought you listed above that kept you from writing, create an alternate thought that you will immediately use to replace it.

Action-Oriented Replacement Thought

Successful writers write no matter what. Even though conditions aren't ideal, I need to stick to my schedule.

Or:

My goal is to write for one hour every night. That's how I will make writing a habit.

Your turn: _____

_____

_____

_____

_____

_____

_____

_____

_____

_____

_____

Now post your resistance-battling thoughts next to your schedule and goals near your computer or in your agenda book. Every time you feel resistance creeping in when it's time for you to get your writing accomplished, pull out your list and reread it. Say the action-oriented replacement thoughts out loud if you need to. Use the words to propel you to your desk.

Distractions are an inevitable part of working as a writer. Follow successful writers' examples and maximize the precious time to write that you've written on your calendar by posting your writing schedule. Use that posted schedule to reinforce the policy that you should not be interrupted except in a true emergency. Eliminate the urge to check e-mail or Internet surf by disconnecting the programs while you write. Remember, you want to make writing the habit when you sit down at your desk, not composing e-mail. Plan ahead for activities like shopping, errands, and other duties that you know must be done. Discipline yourself to not answer the phone or doorbell when you're writing. Last, and most important, reward yourself when you accomplish your writing goals for the day.

chapter fifteen

The Write Frame of Mind

*S*o far we've taken a look at practical strategies that have led to success—strategies like working a schedule, setting goals, creating a Writing Action Plan, treating writing like a job, dealing proactively with distractions, and commandeering writing space in the home. But what *internal* mindsets have successful writers, such as bestselling author Pamela Morsi, cultivated over time that have helped them persevere with their writing? What *thinking* strategies have they used to get results? In other words, what keeps successful writers keepin' on?

In this chapter, I'll give you the answers.

Writer First, *Published* Writer Second

In Chapter 2, you learned that many successful writers write because they love books, reading, and the written word. They don't necessarily start out with the dream of becoming published. Successful writers have turned their love of books, reading, and writing into an opportunity to improve their craft. They are writers first, *published* writers *second*. Writing is the priority.

Novelist Marie Bostwick wrote for a decade before she was published, and she says that focusing on her writing—not the outcome—was what helped lead to her success. Because Bostwick did not have publication as a goal, she developed an ideal strategy for improving her craft, one that you can adopt immediately. "I started out writing a short story a month for about three years," she says. "I did not try to publish them. I was trying to learn to write. I still have these thirty short stories in my possession, and I've given my children instructions that upon my death they are to be burned. They're not published because I knew they weren't ready. They're not fit to see the light of day. And there's nothing wrong with that, but I learned something from every single one of them."

> **"I was driven to tell stories from a very young age, and I wanted so much to keep doing it, and get paid for it, that I refused to give up."**
>
> Tess Gerritsen, *New York Times* bestselling author

The reason the "writer first, published writer second" mindset is so important is because rejection is common to writers, and it can take a while to learn the craft and start getting published. "I think the big question any writer needs to ask her/himself is, 'How much do you want/need to go on writing?'" says novelist Hilary Norman. "If you really want it, the only answer is to go on, work harder, be determined, don't give up."

Reviewing your writing goals on a regular basis and working your Writing Action Plan will help you stay focused and determined. The only requirement to be a writer is a Burning Desire to Write. You have that Burning Desire already. Now put your passion into action.

Happiness Is Writing

Successful writers love to write. The act of writing for them evokes joy and fulfillment (although there are days that the joy comes after the writing is finished). Ironically, it carries them to the top of Maslow's hierarchy even as they move it to the bottom with their other must-do daily tasks. Writing stills the restlessness that so many authors feel when they don't write.

This love of writing also creates the discipline necessary to motivate writers to work on a consistent basis. "I started writing a novel, and I found myself looking forward to doing it," says freelancer Erica Manfred, "and discovering that the discipline comes from within. It's basically that you enjoy it so much that you want to do it. You start living in it."

Writing what she loves is a way that career freelancer Laura Fraser also balances the work she does for pay with the work that often springs from her heart. "Balance the writing you do for publication with some of your own writing, because then you have more of a sense of writing what you love," she says. "It also keeps your writing sharp and it leads to new ideas. So in between writing stories for $2.50 a word, I'll write essays that I get paid hardly anything for, just because I want the satisfaction of writing my own piece of work."

Indulge in your passion and return to the type of writing that you truly enjoy. What kind of writing made you realize that you possessed this Burning Desire deep in your soul? That's the kind of writing you were born to do. Therein lies your passion, your success, and your unique perspective. Practice it, improve your craft, and remain committed to your vision of becoming a successful writer. You will get there.

Adopt a No-Quit Attitude

Writers who find success take perseverance to the extreme by adopting a no-quit, never-give-up attitude. This no-quit attitude pays off. "Writers have to pursue what they want to do and hope that whatever is supposed to happen will," says novelist Pamela Morsi. "Some people will write twenty novels that were never published and they're just under the bed, and suddenly they make a breakthrough and everybody wants their old stuff."

Novelist Lori Handeland experienced precisely that. "I believed I could write and I wasn't going to quit. By the time I sold my first book, I had four completed. I sold them all," she says.

Cultivate your no-quit attitude by working your writing schedule, tracking your progress toward your short-term-quota goals (they really add up!), and continually reviewing your long-term goals. Keep your Vision of Success firmly in the forefront of your mind.

Remember, successful writers write no matter what. What sets successful writers apart is that even when a particular project doesn't sell, successful writers keep going. Adopting a no-quit attitude empowers you to accept responsibility for and take charge of your writing dreams, and a stance of perseverance will serve you in good stead throughout your writing career because even after publication there are obstacles that can hinder a writer's success if she allows them to: "After I'd published eight books, my publisher let me go," says novelist Lori Handeland. "I spent a year trying to sell again. When I did, I sold seven books in the next six months. Even when I'm not under contract, I'm working on something. I don't like to get out of the habit of writing."

Believe in Yourself

A foundational strategy that so many successful writers have employed over the years is belief in self. You have to know you can make it as a writer. You must cultivate your Vision of Success and hold it firmly in mind because that is what fuels belief in self. When you can visualize yourself as a successful writer, you'll *Act as if* you are one, and that will eventually produce results.

You have to believe that you can become successful as a writer. Nurture that image, even on days when it may feel like you're getting nowhere. Believing in yourself and that you can make it is a key to persevering.

Freelance fitness writer Karen Asp says that for her, getting published in *Shape* magazine was initially her primary aspiration. "I remember sitting in my office way back when, looking out the window, trying to get myself established, and thinking, 'I can write these articles that are in *Shape*, I know I can,'" she says. Asp says she didn't doubt that she would get published in *Shape*, it was just a question of when. She kept sending queries and eventually became a contributor to the magazine.

Many successful writers have also had to deflect comments from other people who imply that their dream of becoming a successful author is out of reach. Novelist Carla Neggers experienced this in the beginning of her career, before she got published, and she says that she sees naysayers stopping a lot of aspiring writers in their tracks. "What I see a lot of writers facing is, 'Do I know enough to have written a novel?,' 'Am I good enough?'

and, 'How dare you?'" she says. "I remember the people who would say, 'Being a published author is a pipe dream.' I got told that often. So try to put those kinds of doubts from other people and your own doubts aside and just submit something."

Sometimes those comments from naysayers spur a writer to action. Novelist Kathy Carmichael says she got a virtual kick in the behind to start her writing career after her naysayer called to her through a book. "I used to read a lot of books about writing. One book stated that most writers only pay lip service to writing and never actually finish a book. I took it as a direct slur and didn't want to be one of *those* kinds of writers," she says. Carmichael used the comment as motivation to sit down and write for two days virtually nonstop. The revised version of that writing session became her second published novel.

Climb Your Personal Mountain

Exercising self-discipline and doing what you have to do to meet your long-term goal is a feat that is required of any human in any endeavor. Just like athletes train sometimes for years to reach the top of their sport, you can't expect yourself to achieve your long-term aspirations of finding success as a writer quickly or without sustained effort over a long period of time.

Just as reaching your goals is like climbing the staircase steps one at a time, so becoming a successful writer is like climbing a mountain; to get to the top, you must start at the bottom. So you climb a bit, you get tired, you stop and rest, and the next day you climb some more. You push yourself to get a little further on days that you feel you can do that. With each passing day there is more space between you and the ground and less space between you and the top. You never waver in your belief that you are going to reach the top, even on days when it's cloudy and you can't see it.

"Walk into a library or a bookstore and stand there and look at that mountain range of others who've climbed their personal mountain," says novelist Rick Mofina. "It's being done all the time, it's being done the very moment when you're standing there. The only person preventing you is you."

If you need help believing in yourself as a writer, go back to your writing goals and review them. Look at your goal tracking sheets as a way of priding yourself on how much effort you're making on a regular basis toward your dream. Post these tracking sheets beside your computer as a visual reminder of your perseverance. Reward yourself for writing, celebrate small successes, and give yourself credit for all that hard work.

Psychology 101: Develop an Internal Locus of Control

As we grow up, we learn to perceive the world in a certain way. Early on in life, we begin to form opinions about how much control our actions have over what happens to us in life. The opinions come from our experiences as children. Does our behavior create the results we want, or are we ineffective in the world? This is the theory behind Locus of Control: are we in control of what happens to us or not? The irony is whichever way you think, you're right.

In the simplest terms, people who believe that their own actions influence events and the shape of their lives have an internal Locus of Control, while those with an external Locus of Control believe that fate or other factors outside of their influence control their destinies. In general, people with an internal

Locus of Control have higher self-esteem, they achieve more because they believe they can do so, and they are typically self-directed. As you might guess, most creative high achievers have an internal Locus of Control. They believe that what they do or don't do has a direct impact on how events turn out. And the really funny part is, it doesn't matter if they're right or not. What matters is what they *believe.*

This is why nurturing your Vision of Success and *Acting as if* can be so beneficial in facilitating your success as a writer—the more you think you are successful, the more you'll behave that way, the more you'll take action that causes results. Results lead to feeling more in control of the outcome and leads you to the belief that *yes, I am effective; what I do or don't do has a direct impact on the outcome of this situation.* This makes you feel more in control, and feeling more in control over the outcome inspires more action. Actions lead to results. Results lead to success. Success creates more success. It's a circular, win-win situation.

The good news is even if you don't have an internal Locus of Control about writing you can create one. It all starts with how you think and those messages you send to yourself. That's why they need to be positive. To start developing an internal Locus of Control, acknowledge that you are largely in charge of whether or not you become successful as a writer.

There are factors that you obviously cannot control—whether your book gets accepted or rejected, for instance. But there are many, many factors that you can control. If your book gets rejected, you can control how you feel about that. You can tell yourself that it only takes one yes to get published. You can tell yourself that you'll use that rejection to improve the book and make yourself a better writer. You can tell yourself that eventually the book will get published. You can take small steps like setting and keeping your writing schedule, creating achievable goals and making consistent effort toward those, and working your Writing Action Plan. All of these strategies help strengthen, or create, an internal Locus of Control.

Impose Deadlines on Yourself to Avoid Goof-off-itis

Another way to develop an internal Locus of Control with regard to your writing is by using those deadlines we talked about earlier. This is a common self-disciplinary measure that successful writers used prior to getting published to ensure that they would write consistently. These self-imposed mandates motivate them to act on their own behalf and represent a physical manifestation of their belief that the outcome of their effort is directly related to their action.

Use your short-term-quota goals as your deadlines. It's that simple. You want to finish ten pages of your novel by Saturday? Then Saturday is your deadline. Put it down in red ink on your calendar, and figure out how much work you've got to do to meet that deadline.

Novelist Lori Handeland wrote her first book when she was pregnant with her second child; she finished her book in August, and her son was born in September. She says that experience taught her to always give herself a deadline, and she used short-term-quota goals to do it. "In that way, I learned how to make a deadline by dividing my work into reasonable chunks and completing them every day," she says.

Creating self-imposed deadlines is a helpful strategy to have in your time-to-write toolbox, because all humans suffer from goof-off-itis. Even though writing is going to make you feel great once you get it done for the day, you procrastinate. Your hour of writing has arrived, but you succumb to the oh-so-luring temptation of putting fertilizer on your front lawn. You pop in your new *Sex and the City* DVD. You suddenly take an immense interest in hunting for loose change beneath the cushions on the sofa. Goof-off-itis is a condition of human nature, and you must simply be aware of it and work to overcome it when you're in its clutches. Giving yourself a deadline via your short-term-quota goals creates a certain mindset: writing is important. You have a writing schedule, you have writing goals, and using deadlines creates the expectation that you'll live up to those goals.

Even professional writers suffer from occasional bouts of goof-off-itis. "My ideal working day is to have nothing else to do," says novelist Hilary Norman. Since that's impossible, Norman says she simply starts writing as soon as she can and goes for as long as she can. "I give myself personal, mini-deadlines throughout the writing process," she says.

Setting self-imposed deadlines is a useful technique for nonfiction freelance writers too. If you're working on a magazine query, give yourself a deadline to finish it even though no one is waiting on the other end for it to arrive (and no editor is ever twiddling her thumbs, waiting for more queries!). Deadlines create a sense of urgency about a project and generate internal motivation to get the work done. "I've often, in cases where I was writing something on speculation or an essay, given myself a deadline and taken it as seriously as if someone else had imposed it on me," says freelance writer Greg Daugherty. "I think that helps. If you know you have no choice but to sit down and write something, a lot of the excuses evaporate."

A deadline is a useful tool for focusing the mind, and it's good practice for when you begin to sell your article ideas and have someone waiting for your submission. The worst thing that most writers think they could do is miss a deadline because they had just goofed off. "I've never taken on an assignment with the idea that I wouldn't complete it," says freelancer Randy Southerland. "No matter what, I'd do what I had to do to get it done. I think that's a big part of being a writer, is you have the attitude that there's no excuse for not making the deadline."

Positive Thinking Pays Off

Another important element for developing an internal Locus of Control is to keep your thoughts moving in a positive vein at all times. This is why those positive messages I've encouraged you to start telling yourself are so important. If you believe that your actions will bring about results that you desire, they will.

Since it's a lot easier to think negatively than to think positively, this will likely take conscious effort. Force your attention off what you cannot control—rejection, how many weeks will pass before you get a response to a submission, or how you missed your writing time because the car got a flat tire—and on to those factors that you can control—how many pages per day you turn out, how many queries you send out in a month, or how you can make up that lost writing time once your car is repaired (hey, why not write while you're waiting for the mechanic to fix it?).

"Try not to focus on the things that will make you *stop* writing," says novelist Susan Grant. That is an invaluable piece of advice. Focus on the positive aspects of your writing, the joy it brings you, and revel in the knowledge that you are actively working toward your dream.

Internal obstacles, like lack of belief in yourself and others, don't have to stop you from making time to write. When you create a Vision of Success and hold that image firmly in the forefront of your mind, you can see light at the end of the tunnel. You can see the top of your personal mountain. You know what the end result of that time will be. When you feel yourself slipping, or getting frustrated or discouraged, pull out your goal progress sheets and review them. Delight in how much work you're putting into your dream. Foster your internal Locus of Control by focusing on those aspects of writing that you can control. Believe that your actions will have a direct impact on the outcome. Reward yourself for being one of those rare individuals who actually set, work toward, and reach their long-term aspirations.

chapter sixteen

Rejection Advice from the Pros

*T*he idea of rejection stops many would-be writers from making time to write. Putting yourself out there to the world is scary. It takes guts. Submitting ideas and stories to editors and agents you've never met can be a terrifying endeavor. It takes courage, and lots of it. If you're already doing this, you're to be congratulated for your bravery.

Most aspiring writers know that rejection is inevitable, but it's not easy to take, even when you expect it. Many times aspiring writers take it personally, as if it's a sign that their writing, and subsequently they, are not good enough. Let's take a look at how professional writers, like bestselling author Roxanne St. Claire, cope with rejection.

Don't Take It Personally

It's important to put rejection in its proper perspective. Yes, it hurts, but looked at the right way, it can be something you learn from and use to improve your craft. Rejection isn't an experience that only aspiring writers encounter. Even successful and widely published writers like novelist Merline Lovelace still experience their share of it. "You can't take it personally," she says. "A lot of writers get so discouraged by rejection, so discouraged. But it's a business. I still to this day get rejections."

Rejection is probably more common when writers are first starting out, and at that point it's harder not to take it personally because you don't have a foundation of success to stand on. But continuing to work toward your goal pays off, because you get better as you practice. "When you're starting out, it's very personal. You really link it to your self-esteem, and you can think, 'I'm a terrible writer.' But you get better as you go along," says freelancer Sally Abrahms.

So turn your rejections into an opportunity to improve your writing skills. Remember, creative high achievers strive to constantly learn and grow. And viewing rejection as an opportunity rather than a kick in the pants is how you strengthen your internal Locus of Control. Make the story better and send it out again.

Review, Redo, and Resubmit

Freelance writer Georgia Richardson suggests a three-R approach to rejection letters. "If an editor turns you down, do the three Rs: Review it, redo it if necessary, and then resubmit it," she says. You never know what might happen in the interim. Sometimes a fresh pair of eyes looking at your story is all it takes. Richardson says that at one point she submitted a piece to a national magazine and they turned it down. She waited another month, made a few changes, and resubmitted the article. The previous editor was gone, the new editor loved it, and the piece was published.

Another way to use this approach is to send the editor another idea immediately upon receiving the rejection. So as soon as you receive a rejection letter, send off another query immediately. "I turned right back around and sent them another idea. It was a constant being persistent but not pesky," says freelancer Karen Asp.

Sending out more queries immediately upon rejection is a common strategy among professional writers. It's also a way to turn rejection into a more positive experience. "I turned all rejection into hope. The day I received a rejection letter, I sent out another submission," says novelist Roxanne St. Claire. "My rejections almost all came from agents. So I kept five alive at all times. If I received a rejection, before the sun went down I had another query or partial in the mail to the next agent on the list. At all times, someone had my work under consideration. That way, no matter who rejected it, there was still a chance that the next one would offer representation."

Freelancer Greg Daugherty advises that if you keep pitching ideas to the same magazine and repeatedly get rejected, you may want to step back and assess whether your ideas or writing technique are a match for them. Sometimes how you write may not fit with what an editor is looking for in style. This is where you can practice learning from rejection rather than taking it personally and getting discouraged. "If you've been unsuccessful breaking into a particular market or a particular magazine, that may mean your material isn't right for them or they aren't buying anything from anybody," says Daugherty.

"You have to become immune to the word no. I've learned that no really just means, 'try again later.'"

Gemma Halliday, award-winning author of the *High Heel Mysteries*

"Who knows. You might want to try some other market which may welcome you with open arms."

Fiction writers can use this advice as well. If you're trying to break in with a handful of agents or one publisher and your repeated efforts over time do not result in the outcome you want, try placing your work elsewhere. "A writer needs to be flexible and willing to open her mind to different ways of doing things," says novelist Kathy Carmichael. "In my case, I had targeted one specific publisher and kept trying, and almost succeeding, for years, and they kept my books for years too. Finally, I sent a book to another publisher and they bought it within two weeks. This was a real 'duh' moment for me."

> **"If you're not getting rejected on a fairly regular basis, you might not be trying hard enough to break into new or higher markets."**
>
> Tim O'Shei, freelance writer and editor

It's probably not a good idea to send an onslaught of queries or story ideas to the same publication, editor, or agent. While there's no rule of thumb on this, strive to achieve balance between vigorous submitting and not getting branded as a pest. As Asp advised, be persistent—not pesky.

Believe in Your Story

Here's where believing in yourself and what you have to say is important. If you believe in your story, that will motivate you to submit it multiple times, which is often all it takes to find success. Remember, perseverance is required. "If you believe in a story, if you know it's a good story, you can pitch it elsewhere," says freelance writer Jennifer Haupt. "There's stories I've pitched three or four places over a year."

Not taking rejection personally and believing in your story enough to keep it circulating even after rejection is a key strategy that freelance writer and author Kathryn Lance employs. "I think with fiction even more than nonfiction, you have to *believe* in your story so much that you just keep putting it out there till it finds a home," she says.

Remember: believe in yourself. "I think it takes more guts than anything else to write fiction," says novelist Charlene Ann Baumbich. "I think it's a surrendering to everything that you know that you think to be reasonable, including that you think you can't write. You have to surrender that and just write."

Take the Long View

The key to making time to write over a long enough period to gain success is to take a long view of the writer's process and the writer's journey. Remember: the one who has to believe you can make it is you. "The most horrible thing when you're unpublished is everybody says, 'Have you been published?' as though that's what makes you a writer, instead of the act of writing," says novelist Marie Bostwick. "I think the biggest thing for me was I just had to get over everybody else's expectations and focus on my expectations."

Novelist Jodi Picoult says that taking the long view motivated her to write a second book as she circulated her first. It also helped her keep going after receiving rejection letters. "I got over one hundred rejections from agents, but I kept sending the manuscript out to new ones," she says. "When the first one didn't sell, I wrote a second. I am tenacious, and I've always believed that I knew how to tell a story. I always say selling a book is like selling a house—the whole world doesn't have to like it, but one person must love it. If you think that you've got something that sets you a cut above the rest, one day an agent or editor might wonder why you think that—and take a second look."

Train yourself not to take rejection personally. Don't let it sidetrack you from working your schedule for more than a day. Keep going, and honor your Burning Desire to Write. All it takes is one yes.

chapter seventeen

Ignite Your Burning Desire

y now, you've learned effective tools and techniques to find time to write. You've seen professional writers demonstrate how they overcome obstacles that attempt to usurp that time. You've learned how to tap into a bottomless well of ideas that will make your writing time fruitful. But how do you maintain enthusiasm to make time to write over the long haul?

In this chapter, bestselling authors such as Eloisa James share how the inspiration of other writers can keep the flame of your Burning Desire to Write strong. Whether it's reading the work of writers you admire, attending conferences, or joining a critique group, other writers can have a positive influence on you, support you as you improve your craft, and help keep your enthusiasm high.

Study Your Genre
You've probably heard the advice about reading in your genre as a way to improve your craft. Successful writers take that advice

to the next level by studying the books that they want to emulate. This is an excellent way to teach yourself the craft of writing, and it's a legitimate use of your writing time.

Find a book by an author you admire. Read it once, then skim it a second time and take notes. Outline the book and try to recreate the story's arc. Pull out the main plot points that the author used in each chapter. How did she open the chapter? How did she close it? What are the distinguishing traits of each character that the author highlights as a way of making that character come alive in your mind?

> **"Keep thinking on your topic, because everything you read, if you think you can do better, you can."**
>
> Tara Dillard, professional garden designer and freelance writer

After you've done that, you should have a skeleton outline of the story, similar to what the author might have created. Study that outline to get pointers on how the author constructed her book.

This is a technique that many authors who went on to write bestsellers used when they were first starting out. "I figured out how [authors I liked] did it, and then I just did it," says novelist Eloisa James.

You can also try this technique I learned when I took a sales-letter writing class. As part of an assignment, I had to choose one letter from a book of letters that had been highly successful in generating revenue. I had to then write that letter, by hand and verbatim, ten times. The idea was that actively copying out the material was a better learning technique than passively reading it.

I have to admit that copying out the letter so many times did help me understand the concepts the course was teaching.

Copying out the material is an active rather than passive learning experience, which facilitates understanding.

This works for magazine articles too. Find a magazine that you want to publish in and copy one article word for word. You can do this by hand or on the computer. Take note of how many sources the author quoted. How many sidebars, or information boxes, are provided? How many studies did the writer pull from? Approximately how many words is the article and where in the magazine is it placed? Articles in the front and back are usually shorter and easier for new writers to get assignments in. Studying individual articles this way gives you an idea how to not only break into the magazine, but also how to write the actual articles that the magazine is already publishing.

Attend Conferences

Nothing generates enthusiasm like groups. Remember pep rallies from your high school days? That's a good way to look at writing conferences—they're an opportunity for you to network, meet other writers, learn about the publishing business, and improve your craft.

Conferences are good for making connections with other writers. "It's important to have a community for support, someone you can talk to who shares the same kinds of problems and delights that all authors share," says Barbara Campbell, the author of *Heartwood*. Joining a community of writers to share the ups and downs of being an aspiring author can be helpful to get you through some of the tough times.

Conferences offer the opportunity to learn new skills and bring fresh energy to the projects you're working on back home. "I try to attend one conference a year," says freelancer Christie

Taylor. "Whether it's a conference where I can network, or even just a workshop, I try to take some classes every once in a while in a genre I don't usually do."

You can also meet editors and agents there. Freelancer Tim O'Shei, who also works as an editor, shares a useful tip on how to capitalize on this aspect of writing conferences. In the editors' and agents' workshops, he says, take note of what type of material they are buying, then follow up with them later, once they're back at their offices, rather than at the actual conference. Send them an e-mail later that week. That way they have more opportunity to listen to your idea, because at conferences, editors' and agents' attention is usually in high demand.

Join or Form a Supportive Critique Group

When you get together with other aspiring writers to discuss works in progress, it generates enthusiasm and builds a sense of community. Many writing organizations offer critique groups or local chapters where members can get together to review each other's work. See Appendix A for a list of some major writing organizations.

When looking for a group to join, make sure that the other members have similar goals to yours and that they write in your genre. Ensure that feedback is constructive and useful, not destructive in nature. The point of a critique group is to help everyone improve his or her craft. The one you join should serve that purpose.

Also, keep the advice in perspective. Just because one person says there's a problem with your story doesn't mean that's necessarily true. "Reading a book is really subjective," says novelist Christine Feehan. "If you have four people who say you have major problems with it, then you probably do. Go back and look it over, and don't love it so much that you can't take it apart and see any flaws in it. But if it's one person, don't let it break your heart, because that one person could very well just not like that particular story. It's a 'no' for them."

Some groups designate a leader to help keep the group focused and on track. "I think it's good to participate in a group that has a moderator, and there have to be rules set. The rules are that the critique is for constructive criticism. Constructive is the key word there," says Geri Taran, a cofounder and current president of the Georgia Writer's Association. Additional rules should be set up about how much work and how often a member can submit work for review, how many minutes the others will be given to provide feedback, if work must be submitted before or during the group, and so forth.

To keep your enthusiasm at its peak, make sure you have your writing pep rally from time to time, whether indirectly by reading the inspiring works of others, or directly by attending writing conferences and critique groups. It will give you that extra boost you need to find time to write.

> **"Just about everything with my writing career is very purposeful."**
>
> Debbie Macomber, *New York Times* and *USA Today* bestselling author

chapter eighteen

Your Time-to-Write Toolbox

*Y*ou've now heard from an extensive range of bestselling and professional writers. You've heard the stories, strategies, schedules, goals, and mindsets that these writers use to make time to write. You've learned that anybody who exercises enough self-discipline to carve out the time to write on a consistent basis can become a successful writer.

In this final chapter, you'll hear from bestselling authors like Mary Jo Putney about the importance of believing in yourself as a writer, how developing your own style is critical to success, and how the Burning Desire to Write brings the ultimate satisfaction to writers. We'll conclude with a writing success checklist.

Believe That What You Have to Say Is Important

As I mentioned numerous times throughout this book, successful writers believe in themselves and value what they are doing. They believe that their unique slants, voices, and perspectives are worth putting out to the world. Even if they had to work at it at first, they come to believe that what they have to say is important. "It's easy to believe that what you do doesn't matter, but you have to think that it does matter," says novelist Mary Jo Putney, "that you have stories to tell, and a right to tell them. You should take the time to yourself to explore this ability. You'll always be sorry if you don't do it."

Remember, the only requirement to be a writer is a Burning Desire to Write, coupled with the dedication that that desire naturally creates. Follow that desire up with action and nothing will keep you from success.

As you move ahead with your writing journey, remember to keep your dream alive inside you at all times. Fantasize about the writing you want to do, where your books or articles will appear, how your byline will read. Remember that visualization is a powerful tool that many bestselling authors utilized before they became successful. Get your writing dream down to the smallest detail. Picture the covers of your books, or how your articles will appear in magazines.

Strengthen your resolve to succeed by working your Writing Action Plan. Don't let yourself down by abandoning your goals. Declare your intention to be a writer, and work toward that goal a little bit every day. Remember, even five minutes of writing a day adds up over time. Success is built slowly, but it is cumulative in nature.

Above all else, believe in your abilities to become successful as a writer. Let your love of writing and the joy you find in it carry you toward your dreams. If you keep at it, you will get there. "My need to write is number one," says novelist Tara Taylor Quinn, "followed by determination, ability to visualize, and ability to manifest." You manifest your dream through action.

Let your unique voice emerge. You have something special to bring to the world. You have something to say that no one else has ever said before. "Find your strength and make it work for you," says novelist Rhonda Pollero.

How you find your strength in writing is by writing. You literally write your way to it. It takes time, patience, and perseverance, but finding your strength as a writer and your unique voice are two of the sweetest rewards for consistently finding time to write. "If I have learned one thing in this business, it is that talent will carry you so far, but a great voice will carry you through a career," says novelist Julia London. "Developing your unique voice doesn't happen overnight either. It takes time and practice and thousands and thousands of words for it to shine through."

> "Find the time when your writing juices are flowing. When you find it, guard it like the dickens."
>
> Merline Lovelace, *USA Today* bestselling author

Write what you feel passionate about and that's what will keep your Burning Desire to Write ignited. "When I latched on to health and nutrition, it ignited a passion in me because I felt I was helping people," says freelancer Martin Zucker. "I've been able to interview some of the great healers and pioneers and translate their ideas and messages into words and books and articles that are intended to help people. That's an uplifting mission."

Your Time-to-Write Toolbox

Here are the effective traits, techniques, and strategies of writers who find time to write:

- They have a Burning Desire to Write.
- They create a Vision of Success.
- They create a writing schedule and stick to it.
- They set goals.
- They work a Writing Action Plan.
- They balance sacrifice with reward.
- They commandeer writing space in the home or acquire alternate work space.
- They deal proactively with distractions whenever possible.
- They enlist their families' support as much as possible by posting their schedules and involving their families in the writing process.
- They treat writing like a job, even before it's a paid job.
- They turn all rejection to their advantage.
- They bust through writer's block and the inner critic using time-tested mental strategies.
- They take a break when they genuinely need one.
- They tap into their subconscious minds for ideas and inspiration.
- They use visualization and positive thinking to motivate them to make time to write.
- They *Act as if* they are a successful, working writer before they actually are one.

The End . . . and Your Beginning

The choice to make time to write is yours. I have given you the strategies and techniques of 104 bestselling authors and professional writers that you can apply to your own life in order to create time to write. I've given you ways to make that time no matter what your daily life involves. I've shown you the power of a schedule and of setting writing goals. I've demonstrated that the more you use a schedule, the more writing becomes a good habit.

> **"The number one thing you must do is write. You have to write, write, write, and when you can't write anymore, write some more."**
>
> Steve Berry, *New York Times* bestselling author

You have seen how dozens of bestselling writers like Sandra Brown and Wendy Corsi Staub got where they are today. They shared their stories with me, so I could share them with you.

With all this powerful insider knowledge at your command, what does it take to become a successful writer? Look in the mirror, and you will see.

Happy Writing.

National Writers Organizations

American Society of Journalists and Authors, Inc.
www.asja.org

The Authors Guild, Inc.
www.authorsguild.org

Cat Writers' Association, Inc.
www.catwriters.org

Dog Writers Association of America, Inc.
www.dwaa.org

The Dramatists Guild of America, Inc.
www.dramaguild.com

Garden Writers Association of America
www.gardenwriters.org

Horror Writers Association
www.horror.org

Mystery Writers of America
www.mysterywriters.org

Romance Writers of America
www.rwanational.org

Science Fiction and Fantasy Writers of America, Inc.
www.sfwa.org

Sisters in Crime
www.sistersincrime.org

Society of Children's Book Writers and Illustrators
www.scbwi.org

Text and Academic Authors Association, Inc.
www.taaonline.net

National Association of Science Writers
www.nasw.org

National Writers Union
www.nwu.org/nwu

Novelists, Inc.
www.ninc.com

Western Writers of America
www.westernwriters.org

Online Resources for Aspiring Writers

Absolute Write (*www.absolutewrite.com*) offers advice on writing and getting published to writers in all genres.

Freelance Writing (*www.freelancewriting.com*) has articles and advice for aspiring freelance writers.

In the Company of Writers (*www.inthecompanyofwriters.com*) offers teleseminars and Webinars on all categories of writing.

The Easy Way to Write (*www.easywaytowrite.com*) provides how-to advice on all genre writing, motivational tips, and advice on publishing and marketing your work.

The Fiction Writer's Journey (*www.thefictionwritersjourney.com*) offers resources for fiction writers.

The Practicing Writer (*www.practicing-writer.com*) supports the craft and business of writing and provides links to other newsletters that help aspiring writers.

The Well-Fed Writer (*www.wellfedwriter.com*) is a site that features "income-boosting resources for commercial writers."

Worldwide Freelance Writer (*www.worldwidefreelance.com*) has articles, markets, news, and resources for freelancers.

The Writers Weekly (*www.writersweekly.com*) site provides helpful advice to aspiring writers as well as markets and e-books on publishing and writing.

Writing Career (*www.writingcareer.com*) provides links to resources for all writers, including fiction, copywriters, and screenwriters, and provides information on the publishing process.

Writing Etc. (*http://filbertpublishing.com*) features tips, techniques, and resources to transform you from an average freelancer to a highly paid professional.

Writing on the Run (*www.writingontherun.com*) offers advice for busy aspiring writers on the go.

Writing-World.com (*www.writing-world.com*) is listed as one of *Writer's Digest* best sites for writers, and this newsletter provides advice and tips to aspiring authors.

Sabrina Jeffries's Character Checklist (*reprinted with permission*)

Character Checklist

Major Factors	Hero	Heroine
Profession		
Education		
Financial status as child		
Financial status as adult		
Social status as child		
Social status as adult		
Relationship with mother		
Relationship with father		
Social environment as child		
Social environment as adult		
Geographical environment as child		
Geographical environment as adult		

Character Checklist continued . . .

Major Factors	Hero	Heroine
General health as child		
General health as adult		
Personality		
Ways of Knowing		
Age		
Talents/abilities		
Ethnicity		
Interests/obsessions/hobbies		
Physical appearance: hair, eyes, skin, blood type, anomalies (scars, physical disabilities, unusual characteristics)		
Greatest ambition		
Real ambition		
Attitude toward central problem in book		
Reasons for attitude		
Attitude toward opposite sex		
Reasons for attitude		
Attitude toward love		
Reasons for attitude		

Major Factors	Hero	Heroine
Attitude toward marriage		
Reasons for attitude		
Attitude toward children		
Reasons for attitude		
Attitude toward family (not prospective, so much as h/h own)		
Reasons for attitude		
Reasons for attraction to h/h (you can use the following categories or make your own):		
Nature		
Nurture		
Philosophies		
Talents/abilities		
Interests		

Writers' Biographies

Sally Abrahms (*www.sallyabrahms.com*) writes for national magazines, newspapers and Web sites, as well as for corporations. She has published in *Time, Newsweek, Ladies' Home Journal,* and other magazines.

Cherry Adair (*www.cherryadair.com*) is the *New York Times* bestselling author of *Hot Ice* and *White Heat.*

Lynne Alpern (*www.humorbreak.com*) is an award-winning writer who has published hundreds of articles and authored seven books.

Karen Asp (*www.karenasp.com*) specializes in fitness, health, and nutrition. She is *Allure* magazine's fitness columnist and a regular contributor to *Self, Shape, Woman's Day*, and others.

David Axe is a freelance writer and the author of *Army 101* and *War Fix.*

L.A. Banks, who also writes as Leslie Esdaile Banks, (*www.lesliee sdailebanks.com*) is the *New York Times* and *USA Today* bestselling author of romance, suspense thrillers, and paranormal novels.

Beverly Barton (*www.beverlybarton.com*) is a *New York Times* bestselling and award-winning author of over sixty romance and romantic suspense books.

Charlene Ann Baumbich (*www.welcometopartonville.com*) is the author of the *Dearest Dorothy* series and several nonfiction titles. From grocery lists to e-mail, Charlene loves to write.

Renee Bernard (*www.reneebernardauthor.com*) is a freelance writer and author of *A Lady's Pleasure.*

Steve Berry (*www.steveberry.org*) is an attorney and a *New York Times* bestselling author.

Jenna Black (*www.jennablack.com*) is author of the Guardians of the Night series and the Morgan Kingsley series.

Jennifer Blake (*www.jenniferblake.com*) is a *New York Times* best-selling romance author.

Marie Bostwick (*www.mariebostwick.com*) is the award-winning author of *Fields of Gold* and *River's Edge.*

Peter Bowerman is author of *The Well-Fed Writer* and *TWFW: Back for Seconds*, how-to standards in the lucrative field of commercial freelancing.

Alisa Bowman (*www.alisabowman.com*) is a freelance writer and editor who has written for nationally distributed magazines like *Better Homes and Gardens*. She has collaborated on more than fifteen books, including four *New York Times* bestsellers.

Rebecca Brandewyne (*www.rebeccabrandewyne.com*) is a *New York Times* bestselling and award-winning author.

Connie Brockway (*www.conniebrockway.com*) is a *New York Times* and *USA Today* bestselling author and two-time RITA award winner.

Sandra Brown (*www.sandrabrown.net*) is the author of more than fifty *New York Times* bestselling novels.

Lori Bryant-Woolridge (*www.loribryantwoolridge.com*) is the bestselling author of *Hitts & Mrs.*, *Weapons of Mass Seduction*, and other books.

Barbara Campbell (*www.barbara-campbell.com*) is the author of two fantasy novels and twelve musicals.

Kathy Carmichael (*www.kathycarmichael.com*) is an award-winning romantic comedy author.

Robyn Carr (*www.robyncarr.com*) is the RITA award-winning author of over twenty-five novels.

Victor D. Chase (*www.victordchase.com*) is an award-winning author with over thirty years of experience as a science writer. His recent book, *Shattered Nerves: How Science Is Solving Modern Medicine's Most Perplexing Problem*, garnered a 2007 Outstanding Book award from the American Society of Journalists and Authors.

Nancy Christie (*www.giftsofchange.com*) is the author of *The Gifts of Change*. She contributes to *Better Homes and Gardens, Woman's Day*, and others.

Vicki Cobb (*www.vickicobb.com*) specializes in juvenile nonfiction and has more than eighty-five books to her credit.

Jan Coffey (*www.jancoffey.com*) is the pen name of Nikoo and Jim McGoldrick, an award- winning writing team who pen historical, young adult, and nonfiction books.

Catherine Coulter (*www.catherinecoulter.com*) is a *New York Times* and *USA Today* bestselling author who writes historical romance and contemporary suspense thrillers.

Greg Daugherty has juggled simultaneous careers as a magazine editor and freelance writer for more than twenty-five years. As an editor he's worked for *Reader's Digest, Money*, and *Consumer Reports*. As a writer he has contributed to *Smithsonian, Parenting*, and other magazines.

Barbara Delinsky (*www.barbaradelinsky.com*) is the New York Times bestselling author of *Family Tree* and other novels.

Tara Dillard (*www.taradillard.com*) is a nationally award-winning garden designer, lecturer, and author.

Hallie Ephron (*www.hallieephron.com*) is the author of *Writing and Selling Your Mystery Novel: How to Knock 'Em Dead with Style.* She is also coauthor of five Dr. Peter Zak mystery/psychological thrillers.

Christine Feehan (*www.christinefeehan.com*) is the *New York Times* bestselling author of twenty-six novels, including four series.

Stephen Fenichell is a freelance writer whose articles have appeared in *Forbes/FYI, Men's Journal, GQ,* and others. He is sole author of three books and has collaborated on nine others.

Joy Fielding (*www.joyfielding.com*) is the award-winning author of more than a dozen novels.

Nina Foxx (*www.ninafoxx.com*) is the author of several novels, including *Marrying Up.*

Laura Fraser (*www.laurafraser.com*) is a freelance writer and author of the bestselling travel memoir *An Italian Affair.*

Kevin Garrison (*www.kevincreates.com*) is a retired pilot whose professional writing career spans twenty years. He has produced over eight hundred fifty published articles, newspaper and Web site columns, and numerous books.

Tess Gerritsen (*www.tessgerritsen.com*) is an international and *New York Times* bestselling thriller novelist.

Debra Gordon (*www.debragordon.com*) specializes in writing about medical and health issues for consumers and health care professionals.

Sandra J. Gordon (*www.sandrajgordon.com*) is a health and nutrition writer and author of *Consumer Reports Best Baby Products*, and *The Shy Single*. She contributes to *Child*, *Parents*, and other magazines.

Susan Grant (*www.susangrant.com*) is a RITA award winner and *New York Times* bestselling author. She was one of the first women in history to graduate from the United States Air Force Academy.

Carmen Green (*www.authorcarmengreen.com*) began writing in 1994 and has sold more than fourteen books and novellas.

Kristina Grish (*www.kristinagrish.com*) is the author of *The Joy of Text: Dating, Mating, and Techno-Relating*. She has penned essays and features for *Cosmopolitan*, *Women's Health*, and others.

David Groves is the author of *Be a Street Magician!: A How-To Guide*. He has written over six hundred nonfiction articles in his twenty-five-year writing career for such publications as *Harper's Bazaar*, *Mademoiselle*, *McCall's*, and others.

Gemma Halliday (*www.gemmahalliday.com*) started writing fiction in 2002, and after winning several awards as an unpublished writer she won RWA's prestigious Golden Heart award.

Lori Handeland (*www.lorihandeland.com*) is the *USA Today* bestselling author of *Rising Moon* and other novels.

Kathryn Harrison (*www.kathrynharrison.com*) is the *New York Times* bestselling author of several novels, memoirs, a biography, and a collection of personal essays. Her work has appeared in *Vogue*, *O Magazine*, *Salon*, and others.

Arianna Hart (*www.ariannahart.com*) is the author of *Devil's Playground* and other novels.

Jennifer Haupt (*www.jenniferhaupt.com*) frequently contributes health and lifestyle articles to *Reader's Digest*, *Woman's Day*, *Parents*, and others.

Michele Hoover teaches at Boston University and was published in *Best New American Voices 2004*.

Eloisa James (*www.eloisajames.com*) is a *New York Times* bestselling romance author. She teaches English literature at Fordham University.

Sabrina Jeffries (*www.sabrinajeffries.com*) is a *New York Times* and *USA Today* bestselling romance writer.

Linda Winstead Jones (*www.lindawinsteadjones.com*) is the RITA–winning author of more than fifty romance novels and novellas.

Daphne Kalotay (*www.daphnekalotay.com*) is the author of *Calamity and Other Stories*.

Sherrilyn Kenyon (*www.sherrilynkenyon.com*) also writes as Kinley MacGregor and is the *New York Times* bestselling author of *Devil May Cry* and other novels.

Kathryn Lance is author of more than fifty books of fiction and nonfiction for adults and children. Her best-known fiction includes *Pandora's Genes* and *Pandora's Children* (for adults) and *Going to See Grassy Ella* (for middle-school readers).

Joyce and Jim Lavene (*www.joyceandjimlavene.com*) are a married writing team. They are members of Mystery Writers of America, Sisters-in-Crime (local and national), and several local writing groups.

John Lescroart (*www.johnlescroart.com*) is a *New York Times* bestselling author whose books have been translated into sixteen languages in more than seventy-five countries.

Julia London (*www.julialondon.com*) is a *New York Times* and *USA Today* bestselling romance author.

Stephanie Losee (*www.stephanielosee.com*) is a frequent contributor to the *San Francisco Chronicle Magazine* and a regular contributor to the *Los Angeles Times, New York Post,* and Women .com.

Merline Lovelace (*www.merlinelovelace.com*) is a retired colonel from the United States Air Force and *USA Today* bestselling author of more than sixty-five novels.

C.J. Lyons (*www.cjlyons.net*) is a pediatric emergency medicine doctor who writes award-winning medical suspense novels.

Debbie Macomber (*www.debbiemacomber.com*) is the *New York Times* and *USA Today* bestselling author of *Back on Blossom Street* and other novels.

Ann Major (*www.annmajor.com*) is a *USA Today* bestselling author and a founding member of Romance Writers of America.

Erica Manfred (*www.ericamanfred.com*) is a freelance journalist whose reported pieces have appeared in *Self, Consumers Digest, Ladies' Home Journal,* and others.

Kat Martin (*www.katbooks.com*) is a *New York Times* bestselling author of historical romance, contemporary, and romantic suspense novels.

Sandra Marton (*www.sandramarton.com*) is a top author for *Harlequin Presents.*

Rick Mofina (*www.rickmofina.com*) is an internationally bestselling suspense novelist and former journalist.

Pamela Morsi (*www.pamelamorsi.com*) is a *USA Today* bestselling romance author.

Bruce W. Most has been a full-time freelance writer for over thirty years. He has published in numerous national magazines, written hundreds of articles and commercial works, edited a financial planning journal, and ghostwritten a nonfiction book.

Cecil "Cec" Murphey is a *New York Times* and *USA Today* bestselling author who has written or co-written over one hundred books. His two bestsellers are *90 Minutes in Heaven*, written for Don Piper, and *Gifted Hands: The Ben Carson Story*.

Sophia Nash (*www.sophianash.com*) is an award-winning romance writer.

Carla Neggers (*www.carlaneggers.com*) is the *New York Times* bestselling author of *The Widow* and other novels.

Hilary Norman (*www.hilarynorman.co.uk*) is the author of *Compulsion* and other novels.

Jennifer O'Connell (*www.jenniferoconnell.com*) is the author of *Off the Record, Bachelorette #1*, and other books.

Tim O'Shei (*www.timoshei.com*) is the author of more than three dozen books, most of them for young readers. He is a newspaper editor, magazine writer, and former teacher.

Marla Paul (*www.marlapaul.com*) is the author of *The Friendship Crisis: Finding, Making, and Keeping Friends When You're Not a Kid Anymore*.

Carly Phillips (*www.carlyphillips.com*) is a *New York Times* best-selling romance author.

Jodi Picoult (*www.jodipicoult.com*) is the *New York Times* best-selling author of *My Sister's Keeper* and other novels.

Rhonda Pollero (*www.rhondapollero.com*) is a *USA Today* best-selling author who has penned more than thirty novels including the *Rose Tattoo* and the Landry Brothers series (under the pen name Kelsey Roberts). She has received numerous industry awards.

Mary Jo Putney (*www.maryjoputney.com*) is the *New York* Times bestselling author of *A Distant Magic* and other novels.

Jennifer Quasha has written more than forty books for kids and adults. She is a *Dog Fancy* columnist and contributing editor at *Dogs for Kids*.

Tara Taylor Quinn (*www.tarataylorquinn.com*) is the *USA Today* bestselling author of more than forty novels.

Tinker Ready covers health and science for a range of newspapers and magazines. She has written for *Nature Medicine*, the *Boston Globe*, and others. She worked in Washington, D.C., for two years, covering Capitol Hill for *Health Week*.

Kaitlyn Rice (*www.kaitlynrice.com*) is a contemporary romance writer.

Georgia Richardson (*www.queenjawjaw.com*) writes a humor column for *boomer* magazine. She's contributed to *Woman's World*, *Chicken Soup for the Soul Magazine*, and others.

Kimberla Lawson Roby (*www.kimroby.com*) is the *New York Times* bestselling author of *Changing Faces*, *Love & Lies*, and other novels.

Maxine Rock got her B.S. in journalism from New York University and a master's in journalism and science at the University of Michigan. She's written nine nonfiction books, more than one thousand articles, and gathered nineteen awards for journalism excellence.

JoAnn Ross (*www.joannross.com*) is the *New York Times* and *USA Today* bestselling author of *No Safe Place*.

Rachel Safier (*www.theregoesthebride.com*) is a freelance writer and author of *There Goes the Bride*.

Barbara Samuel (*www.barbarasamuel.com*) has earned her way by writing since she was eighteen years old. She has won nearly every award given to romance and women's fiction, including five RITAs, two Colorado Center for the Book awards, and many others. She has appeared on the Walden's and *USA Today* bestseller lists for romance.

Robin Schone (*www.robinschone.com*) is the *USA Today* bestselling author of *Scandalous Lovers*.

Elizabeth Shimer is a freelance writer who specializes in health and women's issues.

Randy Southerland (*www.southwrite.com*) is a Georgia-based freelance writer specializing in business, health care, and travel. His work has appeared in a wide variety of newspapers as well as business, travel, and industry publications.

Wendy Corsi Staub (*www.wendycorsistaub.com*) is a *New York Times* bestselling suspense novelist who is also a bestselling author of women's fiction under the pseudonym Wendy Markham.

Roxanne St. Claire (*www.roxannestclaire.com*) is a *New York Times* and *USA Today* bestselling author of more than a dozen novels of romance, suspense, and women's fiction. Her books have been recognized with numerous industry awards.

Alix Strauss is the author of *The Joy of Funerals*. The book is the recent winner of the Ingram Award and was named Best Debut Novel by *New York Resident* magazine.

Letitia Sweitzer (*www.LetitiaLifeCoaching.com*) has written more than two hundred articles and is a collaborator on seven nonfiction books, as well as poetry and scripts for theatre.

Geri Taran is the cofounder and current president of the Georgia Writer's Association. Her works range from business and corporate publications to stories and poems for both young people and adults.

Christie Taylor (*www.christietaylor.net*) first began writing about her passion, the arts, for the *Boston TAB* and *Boston Herald*, primarily covering dance. Later she freelanced for publications such as the *Houston Chronicle* and *New York Times*.

Vicki Lewis Thompson (*www.vickilewisthompson.com*) is the *New York Times* bestselling author of romantic comedy.

Joan Wolf (*www.joanwolf.com*) is the award-winning author of dozens of novels in the genres of romance, mystery, straight historical, and prehistorical.

Rebecca York (*www.rebeccayork.com*), the pen name of Ruth Glick, is a *New York Times* and *USA Today* bestselling romantic suspense author. She has twice been a RITA finalist and has won three Lifetime Achievement Awards from *Romantic Times Book Club* magazine.

Martin Zucker writes books and magazine articles about health and medicine. He coauthored *Reverse Heart Disease Now* and *Move Yourself.* He is a former Associated Press newsman.

Index

About the Author

Kelly L. Stone is a freelance writer, novelist, and licensed counselor with a master's degree in counseling. Since establishing a writing career while holding down a full-time job, her articles and essays have appeared in *Family Circle, Writer's Digest, Cat Fancy, Chicken Soup for the Soul,* and *A Cup of Comfort®*. Her first novel, *Grave Secret,* was published in August 2007. She is a writing instructor and a frequent presenter at writers' conferences. She lives in Atlanta. Visit her online at *www.kellylstone.com,* or e-mail her at kelly@kellylstone.com.